The Resilience
of Southern Identity

The Resilience of
Southern Identity

*Why the South Still Matters
in the Minds of Its People*

Christopher A. Cooper and H. Gibbs Knotts

The University of North Carolina Press CHAPEL HILL

This book was published with the assistance of the Fred W. Morrison Fund of the University of North Carolina Press.

Set in Espinosa Nova by Westchester Publishing Services
Manufactured in the United States of America

The University of North Carolina Press has been a member
of the Green Press Initiative since 2003.

Library of Congress Cataloging-in-Publication Data
Names: Cooper, Christopher Alan, 1975– | Knotts, H. Gibbs.
Title: The resilience of southern identity : why the South still matters
    in the minds of its people / Christopher A. Cooper and H. Gibbs Knotts.
Description: Chapel Hill : University of North Carolina Press, [2017] |
    Includes bibliographical references and index.
Identifiers: LCCN 2016021185 | ISBN 9781469631059 (cloth : alk. paper) |
    ISBN 9781469652160 (pbk. : alk. paper) | ISBN 9781469631066 (ebook)
Subjects: LCSH: Group identity—Southern States. | Southern States—Civilization. |
    Southern States—Historiography.
Classification: LCC F209 .C636 2017 | DDC 975—dc23 LC record
    available at https://lccn.loc.gov/2016021185

Cover illustration by Craig Evans, Founder, Y'allsome.

This book is dedicated to Whitney, Jack, and Madeline, born in the South, but free to let their southern identity lapse as they see fit.

Contents

Acknowledgments xi

Introduction 1

CHAPTER ONE
The Roots of Southern Identity 10

CHAPTER TWO
Signs of the South 31

CHAPTER THREE
Southern Identity by the Numbers 48

CHAPTER FOUR
Talking with Southerners 69

Conclusion 96

Appendix 107
Notes 117
References 121
Index 131

Maps and Tables

MAPS

  2.1 D score map 41

  2.2 S score map 42

TABLES

  3.1 Southern identity by state 56

  3.2 Comparing the predictors of southern identity in 1992 and 2011 58

  4.1 Focus group participants 72

A1.1 Are foods really regional? 107

A1.2 Is there a difference between white and black food preferences in the South? 108

A1.3 South/Non-South feeling thermometer differences 109

A2.1 Regression models predicting the prevalence of "Dixie" and "Southern" businesses 110

A3.1 Logistic regression models for "Do you consider yourself a Southerner?" 112

A3.2 Logistic regression models for "Explaining regional pride" using Southern Identity Poll (2011) 113

A3.3 Logistic regression models for "Support for the Civil War and the Confederacy" using 2011 Pew Poll 114

Acknowledgments

We've lived nearly all of our lives in the South and have devoted a considerable portion of our academic careers to studying the region. We've been at times proud and ashamed of our southern heritage, and it's the region's contradictions that motivate our interest in the South and the subject of southern identity.

Even with a coauthor, a book project can be a lonely endeavor. We feel very fortunate to have a number of supportive colleagues who have helped us develop our ideas, refine our concepts, and ultimately complete this project. At Western Carolina University, we'd like to express particular thanks to Heidi Buchanan, Todd Collins, Phyllis Hoffman, Don Livingston, Alex Macaulay, Libby McRae, Justin Menickelli, and Richard Starnes. We also want to thank Western Carolina University's Ron Davis for his help creating the maps that appear in chapter 2. At the College of Charleston, we are particularly appreciative of the support from Claire Curtis, Mark Long, Jordan Ragusa, and Kristin Wichmann. We also want to give a special thanks to the College of Charleston's Annette Watson, who pushed us to add a qualitative chapter and helped answer our questions about focus groups, as well as to Kendra Stewart. As director of the Joseph P. Riley Center for Livable Communities, Kendra provided much-needed financial support to move this project forward. We also got helpful research assistance from Emily Wager, and we greatly appreciate the individuals who took the time to talk about their southern identity in our focus groups. Audience members and discussants at the Citadel Symposium for Southern Politics, Southern Political Science Association, and the Auburn University-Montgomery Conference on Southern Studies also helped us sharpen our arguments.

In addition to the folks we name above, we are indebted to the hundreds of scholars who have dedicated much of their careers to the study of southern politics and society. Chief among these is University of North Carolina sociologist, and dean of southern studies, John Shelton Reed. Reed's contributions to this subfield are too numerous to name, and this book could not have been written without the insights we derived from his impressive body of work.

We are also fortunate to have had the support of our editor at the University of North Carolina Press, Chuck Grench, who has advocated for this project from beginning to end. We also appreciate the excellent editorial assistance of Jad Michael Adkins and Iza Wojciehowska, as well as two careful reviews by Winthrop University's Scott Huffmon and the University of North Carolina's Ferrel Guillory.

Finally, we want to thank our immediate and extended families. Jessie Swigger, Stacy Knotts, and Whitney Knotts have read many different versions of our manuscript, providing valuable feedback and pointed critiques along the way. Their support is very much appreciated if not always completely deserved.

The Resilience
of Southern Identity

Introduction

Paula Deen is a southerner. That much never has been, and probably never will be, in doubt. The restaurateur and celebrity chef made her fortune selling an image of a gentile, if overly salted, South. Ultimately, it was her view of the region that eventually undermined her. During a deposition, Deen admitted that she had used racial slurs in the past, and noted that she had wanted to plan a "very southern style wedding" replete with "middle-aged black men" in suits and bow ties (Walker 2013). Deen eventually blamed her southern heritage and upbringing for her transgressions (Collins 2013).

James Clyburn is a southerner. Born in Sumter, South Carolina, to a fundamentalist minister and beautician, Clyburn organized civil rights marches and demonstrations throughout the Palmetto State, meeting his wife Emily while incarcerated for civil disobedience. Despite experiencing the worst of the Jim Crow South as a young African American man, Clyburn devoted his life to public service, working in state politics and eventually rising to the position of Majority Whip of the U.S. House of Representatives. In the epilogue to his memoir, Clyburn (2014, 335) writes to his children and grandchildren, saying, "As Americans and South Carolinians, I hope you are as proudly black and genuinely southern as your parents and grandparents were."

Natasha Trethewey is a southerner. Born in Gulfport, Mississippi, to a white father and African American mother, her collection of poems *Native Guard* won the 2007 Pulitzer Prize, and in 2012, she was named U.S. Poet Laureate. Calling herself both quintessentially southern and American, Trethewey shows that the American experiences of "miscegenation, of border crossings, of integration of cultures" are also part of the southern experience. As she notes in a recent interview, "My role is to establish what has always been Southern, though at other points in history it has been excluded from 'Southernness'" (Turner 2013).

Patterson Hood is a southerner. The lead singer of the rock band the Drive by Truckers once penned a song about "The Three Great Alabama Icons": Crimson Tide football coach Bear Bryant, Lynyrd Skynyrd lead vocalist Ronnie Van Zant, and segregationist politician George C. Wallace

(Hood 2002). For Hood, the region is a changing place. "We're not deny-
ing things that went down," Hood says, "but I think we have taken great
strides in the South" (Colurso 2013). Striking a hopeful tone about the region's future, Hood writes, "If we can continue to move forward (however
slowly though it sometimes seems) and learn from and incorporate the
newer cultures moving into the region, we can truly be the best part of the
country to live in and raise a family" (Hood 2013).

BLACK AND WHITE, male and female, middle-aged and old-aged: Deen,
Clyburn, Trethewey, and Hood are very different people, to be sure. It's
unlikely that any of them have ever crossed paths with the others; in fact,
it's difficult to imagine how, where, or why they would meet each other.
Despite these differences, one thing that unites them is that each identifies
as a southerner.

These vignettes also help us preview the puzzle of southern identity
and lead to three primary questions we explore in this book. First, how
typical are these four individuals? Second, what types of people are most
likely to identify as southerners? And third, why do people from diverse
backgrounds, particularly diverse racial backgrounds, identify with the
South?

The Resilience of Southern Identity

Even the most casual observer of the South would note the sweeping changes
that have occurred within the region since 1950. To name just a few of the
most politically relevant examples: de jure segregation is no longer permit-
ted, black voter registration in the South has risen from just below 20 percent
of the black voting aged population to about 70 percent today (Hood, Kidd,
and Morris 2012), and the composition of southern states' legislatures has
shifted from virtually universal Democratic domination to one where Republicans control every chamber (Cooper and Knotts 2014).

Demographic shifts have also defined the region. The South is the country's most populous geographic region, with over 121 million people (U.S.
Census Bureau 2015). To put this in perspective, about the same number of
people live in the Census South as in the Northeast and Midwest combined.
The last 65 years have witnessed a substantial in-migration of people moving
to the South and a dramatic rise in the region's Hispanic population. The
region has also undergone considerable urbanization, with more than three
quarters of southerners now living in urban areas (up from below 50 percent

in 1950). There are many reasons for the continued growth in population. Quality of life and warmer weather are certainly factors, but southern states also offer a friendly business environment, with lower taxes and fewer regulations than other parts of the country (Kotkin 2013).

The cultural landscape has witnessed similar changes—chain restaurants have replaced individual mom-and-pop diners in many towns, the interstate highway system connects the region to the rest of the country, and advertising has become nationalized. Even the media landscape has shifted—an online version of the *New York Times* can be viewed from anywhere with an Internet connection, and the print version can be purchased throughout the South, even in places like the Ingles supermarket in tiny Sylva, North Carolina.

Given these changes (and this is only a small list), many have argued that southern identity is becoming less important. On the face of it, this is a reasonable argument: Why would people connect with a region whose distinctiveness seems to be fading more each day? As we demonstrate in considerable detail in the pages that follow, however, just the opposite has occurred. Southern identity has weathered these potential challenges quite well. Today's residents of the southern United States are at least as likely to proclaim their southern identity as they ever have been.

Though it may seem counterintuitive, we argue that many of these changes in the political and social world keep regional identification relevant in the twenty-first century. As we explain in chapter 1, regional identity in general, and southern identity more specifically, serves an important purpose in people's lives. Southern identity does not represent just a tacit connection to an ephemeral concept, but rather one that is central to how people organize their values and understand their connections to the physical and social worlds around them. While modernization, under some circumstances, can lead to a decline in regional identity, modernization also creates opportunities for people in the South to interact with people from outside the region (Reed 1983). As a result of this interaction, southerners gain a heightened sense of regional consciousness, which can enhance southern identity. Given that identity is a natural part of who we are, it is not surprising that as things change, our need for connection and identity does not disappear. As historian George Tindall (1976, 21) remarked, "We learn time and time again from the southern past and the history of others that to change is not necessarily to disappear. And, we learn from modern psychology, that to change is not necessarily to lose one's identity; to change, sometimes, is to find it."

As we discuss in chapter 1, many observers of the region have long believed that southern distinctiveness and southern identity are on their way out. Just a few decades after historians, humanities scholars, and sociologists began to examine how the South had developed a unique politics, literature, culture, and manner of thinking (Tindall 1960), subfields of the very same disciplines began to dismiss the idea of a distinct South. Many of these commentators argued that the notion of regionalism and the utility of imagining a distinct South were going the way of the Dodo bird. Consider this passage from 1957: "The happy truth is that the South has lost its 'regional integrity.' The writer of tomorrow must take into account another South, a South already born and growing lustily, a rich South, urban, industrialized, and no longer 'southern' but rather northernized, Europeanized, cosmopolitan" (Westbrook 1957, 234).

Around the same time period, journalist Harry Ashmore (1958) wrote *An Epitaph for Dixie*, implying that the concept of the South as a distinct region was dead and buried. We could list scores of other examples calling for the end of regionalism, but suffice it to say, professional and amateur South-watchers have declared the idea of regions and regional identity on life support for at least half a century. With apologies to Mark Twain, we believe that reports of the South's death have been greatly exaggerated.

To address our third question about why people from diverse backgrounds identify with the South, we focus on the ways southern identity has evolved over time. Though resilient in its intensity, we argue that the nature of southern identity has changed rather dramatically over the last several decades. For many whites, maintaining the region's racial hierarchy is no longer part of what it means to be a southerner. As one historian noted, "in the 1860s white southerners found they could be southern without slavery, and in the 1960s they found they could be southern without white supremacy; many increasingly dare to suggest that the South can survive without the Confederate battle flag" (Carlton 2001, 44). Concurrent with these changes in the nature of southern identity among whites, many blacks have also continued to find reason to connect with the region. This willingness of blacks (a group that has experienced slavery, segregation, and continued discrimination) to identify as southerners is an important piece in the puzzle of southern identity. Historian James Cobb (2005b, 64) provides some historical underpinnings that we will build on throughout this book: "The hard-won advances of the 1950s and 1960s freed many African Americans to embrace their southern roots and celebrate and examine their attachments to southern people and places." Taken together, these changes have produced an environment where southern identity today is no longer synonymous with being white. In fact, blacks today are slightly *more* likely to identify as southerners (Griffin, Evanson, and Thompson 2005), and express *more* positive attitudes toward southerners as a group than do their white counterparts (Black and Reed 1982; Cooper and Knotts 2012a).

For a dwindling, but not inconsequential minority, the "Old South" remains. This is a South of traditional gender roles and a firmly established racial order—one defined more by the Confederate flag and tales of old Dixie than by the integration of African Americans into the political leadership of the region. As evidenced by the horrific 2015 church shooting in Charleston, South Carolina, this form of southern identity can even have violent consequences (Eversley 2015). As reprehensible as the expressions of Old South identification can be, it is clearly less prevalent than it once was, and the reduction in this Old South identification has made way for new types of southern identity to emerge. For some, identification with the South is more about a connection to the region's folkways and to place than it is to policy or ideology.[1] For others still, the contemporary South is all of those things at once—a place where many modern day southerners navigate the region's confusing and omnipresent history. Regardless of how they see the South, however, the majority of today's black and white southerners see themselves as inexorably linked to the region.

Our Strategy

This is a book about how people and place interact. Not everyone who lives in the South considers him or herself to be a southerner, and not everyone outside of the South eschews the southerner label. As a result, we make a distinction between "geographic southerners" and people we simply refer to as "southerners." When we refer to geographic southerners, we mean any individual living in the formal definition of the South, regardless of whether they identify with the region.[2] When we refer to the more generic term, southerners, however, we include any individual who claims at least some level of identity with the region, regardless of whether the individual lives in the Bronx, New York, or Oxford, Mississippi.[3] In fact, one of the people profiled at the beginning of this chapter, Patterson Hood, currently lives in Portland, Oregon—about as far away from the geographic South as you can get and still be in the continental United States (Tissenbaum 2015).

It is important to emphasize that this is not, and was never meant to be, a book celebrating the South. We've lived in the South nearly all our lives, but a starry-eyed merriment toward the region has never appealed to us. In chapter 1 we even argue that southern identity may be used to prime a variety of negative emotions—a phenomenon we call "the dark side of southern identity." To be clear, you won't find any supersized belt buckles in our closets, jacked up trucks in our driveways, or Confederate flags on our properties. It is our conflict with the region, and the time we spent questioning, and later coming to grips with, our own southern identities, that was a primary motivation for writing this book.

We also recognize that the concept of southern identity does not fall neatly within disciplinary lines. As a result, we take an explicitly interdisciplinary approach in the pages that follow. Throughout this book, we cite, quote, and draw upon work by sociologists, geographers, historians, political scientists, rhetoricians, psychologists, and a few folks who do not fit in any of these categories but inform our knowledge of the topic at hand. Some of these people may be traditional academics with university appointments, but others are not professors, but writers, journalists, and observers of the South and its people. In this way, the ideas in this book are as influenced by the journalistic accounts of Tracy Thompson and the fully wrought characters of novelist Ron Rash as they are by the scores of surveys collected by people like John Shelton Reed and Larry Griffin. In the end, we hope that this book, its arguments, and its evidence reflect the academic literature, but are not defined by it.

Just as the study of southern identity does not fall neatly within disciplinary (or even academic) lines, neither does it lend itself naturally to a singular research approach. As a result, we employ what social scientists refer to as a mixed-methods design in this book. Simply put, this means we use many different tools and bases of evidence to further our argument. Some of our evidence is quantitative—meaning that we use numbers to summarize and explain the nature of southern identity today. These quantitative methods allow us to draw general conclusions about the region as a whole, differentiate between competing explanations, and gain insights into how identity has changed over time. While quantitative data are valuable, they do not answer all of our questions, but rather sometimes lead us to search for more description, more detailed explanations, and more context. In these situations, we augment the numbers with a qualitative approach that allows a place for today's southerners to speak for themselves. Sometimes we devote an entire chapter to this qualitative approach, but other times, we sprinkle qualitative evidence throughout a chapter to provide context and explanation to our numbers and analyses.

We make no claim that any particular approach provides the best way to understand southern identity, but we do believe that this mixed-method strategy provides a nuanced and textured way to understand the complexities of regional identification today. Relying on any one of these ways to collect and analyze evidence would have led to a less complete and, ultimately, less compelling understanding of southern identity.

As you might have guessed, there were a lot of choices that went into our data collection and analyses. While some readers might be interested in these details and their implications, we strive to keep the main body of the book free of statistical and social-scientific jargon. As a result, we have placed details of our research methodology in the appendix. We hope this keeps the text clear enough for general readers, but still provides the necessary detail for scholars and others who want to know more about where we got our data and how we arrived at our conclusions.

Chapter Outline

In chapter 1, "The Roots of Southern Identity," we ground our work within the larger context of regional identity before turning our attention directly to the issues of southern identity and southern distinctiveness. We also include some original analyses in this chapter, highlighting the unique role that food and politics play in the southern landscape. We argue that the South remains culturally and politically distinct and that the *perception* of distinctiveness is a particularly important component of southern identity. In addition, we examine the complicated relationship between race and southern identity. We also introduce what we term the "dark side of southern identity," a phenomenon in which politicians play on southern identity of old to prime voters to support populist, exclusionary, and even racist candidates and policies. We then draw on the social identity literature to better understand the reasons someone decides to be a member of a regional group. Last, we end the chapter by revisiting our primary research questions that will guide the chapters that follow.

We examine evidence about the changing nature of southern identity through an analysis of business names in chapter 2, "Signs of the South." We establish that there has been a decline in the frequency of businesses using the name "Dixie" and a slight increase in the number of businesses using the "Southern" moniker. We then provide visual representations of these changes by mapping the results. We also rely on business and economic data to establish that "Dixie" and "Southern" businesses are indeed unique and have very different profiles, and we supplement our findings with interviews of "Dixie" and "Southern" business owners. Taken together, this evidence demonstrates that a general concept of southern identity remains resilient and also that the nature of southern identity is changing—and will likely continue to change.

In "Southern Identity by the Numbers," we explore the changing nature of southern identity more closely by analyzing a host of public opinion surveys on the topic. Much of chapter 3 is focused on the answers to a single question that has been asked time and time again throughout the years: "Do you consider yourself a southerner, or not?" By examining these answers from a number of different angles, we show that geographic southerners have responded in the affirmative with surprising consistency. We also combine answers to this question with demographic characteristics that survey respondents give to provide a profile of people who are more or less likely to consider themselves southerners over time. One key finding of this investigation is that blacks and whites today are equally likely to identify as southerners. Though race does not predict southern identity, we discover that blacks hold different opinions than whites on issues related to important regional symbols. When considered as a whole, the answers to these survey questions suggest that people are constructing their own conceptions of what it means to be a southerner.

In chapter 4, "Talking with Southerners," we present evidence from a series of focus groups. These focus groups allow us to explore southern identity in more detail and follow up on many of the themes that developed in earlier chapters. Our focus-group participants include adult southerners from a variety of backgrounds—young and old, white and black, native and nonnative. We discover many similarities about how blacks and whites think about regional identity and the South. Folkways—like hospitality, manners, pace of life, a connection to the land, and food—are key components of southern identity for both groups. As we found in chapter 3, however, we also found key differences in southern identity across the two groups. The most notable differences have to do with the ways whites and blacks talk about history, politics, and race relations.

We return to our vignettes, address the key questions we outlined in this introduction, and recap the book's primary findings in the conclusion. We also highlight the book's theoretical contributions, building on the social identity literature outlined toward the end of chapter 1. We establish that southern identity remains, but that the shape of twenty-first-century southern identity is different from twentieth-century identity. We close with a discussion of the future of southern identity and then return to our argument about why we think regionalism and regional distinctiveness will only become more pronounced in an increasingly interconnected world.

CHAPTER ONE

The Roots of Southern Identity

On the hot, clear evening of June 17, 2015, a twenty-one-year-old South Carolina native named Dylann Roof, walked into Emanuel African Methodist Episcopal (AME) Church in Charleston, South Carolina, and asked to speak with the Pastor. The Reverend Clementa Pinckney invited the young man to sit down at the long table that formed the physical centerpiece of their weekly bible study. Roof, the only white person in a room of twelve blacks, obliged, but didn't say much or contribute to the discussion that was underway. About an hour after he entered the church, Roof pulled out a .45 caliber Glock semiautomatic pistol that he had concealed in his fanny pack, emptied its magazine, reloaded, and emptied it four more times. By the time Roof fled, he had killed nine people. He escaped, gun in hand, and the manhunt to capture him began soon after. Roof was arrested in Kings Mountain, North Carolina, less than fourteen hours after committing one of the worst terrorist attacks in South Carolina history.

As the details of the attack and the attacker's motivations emerged, it became clear that this was not a random act of violence, but one borne out of racism, and a particularly abhorrent understanding of southern identity. In Roof's mind, this shooting was a defense of a natural racial hierarchy—a racial hierarchy that he connected in part with his identity as a white southerner. One of Roof's high school friends even characterized his penchant for racist jokes as an outward manifestation of "southern pride." Roof took pictures of himself with the Confederate battle flag, and his four-door Hyundai Elantra featured a Confederate States of America license plate on the front bumper.

It is likely because of these views of southernness that Roof chose Charleston, a city over ninety miles from his home in Lexington, South Carolina, as the site to execute a racially charged terrorist attack. Charleston is a beautiful city, but one that is replete with reminders of the region in which it's located. There are museums in buildings where slaves were once sold, and antebellum plantations lie just outside of town. Even the city's famous culinary offerings are undeniably southern, and it's certainly not unusual to see a Confederate flag or two while walking around town. It's also a city that is known fondly as "Holy City," a reflection of both the number of churches in town, and also the reverence with which its residents hold religion.

And perhaps no other place reflects the multiple sides of this city than the Emanuel AME Church. "Mother Emanuel" as many call it, counts Denmark Vesey, the architect of one of the largest slave revolts in U.S. history, among its founders. While the historic church holds a key place in African American history, it sits on a street named for John C. Calhoun, a former politician and political theorist who famously proclaimed on the floor of the U.S. Senate that slavery is a "positive good." Calhoun's body rests about seven blocks away.

As details of the attack were made public and the community came together after the tragic events, another side of the South, and of southern identity, began to emerge. Many observers were moved by the southern hospitality that was extended to Roof when he entered Mother Emanuel. As Felicia Sanders, mother of shooting victim Tywanza Sanders, noted during Roof's first court appearance, "We welcomed you Wednesday night in our Bible study with open arms" (Stewart and Pérez-Peña 2015). The nation also watched in amazement as other members of the victims' families offered forgiveness to Roof, just two days after he committed the attacks. In another moving tribute, thousands of southerners from various racial groups joined hands on the Arthur Ravenel Bridge, forming a "Bridge to Peace." The community's response even caught the attention of President Obama, who spoke in considerable detail about the grace that was displayed in the aftermath of the shootings during his eulogy for Reverend Pinckney.

This tragedy caused many white and black southerners to openly discuss the meaning of southern identity itself. South Carolina Republicans, ranging from Tea Party stalwart Governor Nikki Haley to State Senator Paul Thurmond, grandson of notorious segregationist Senator Strom Thurmond, called for the Confederate battle flag to be removed from the South Carolina State House grounds. Similar sentiments soon spread around the South as Republican governor of Alabama Robert Bentley, Republican governor of North Carolina Pat McCrory, and Republican senator from Mississippi Thad Cochran, among others, called for removal of the flag from some government property in their respective states. Patterson Hood, the musician we profiled briefly in the introduction, responded with a *New York Times* op-ed, standing up for the notion of southern identity, but arguing that "truly honor(ing) our Southern forefathers" can best be accomplished not by flying the Confederate flag, but rather by "moving on from the symbols and prejudices of their time and building on the diversity, the art and the literary traditions we've inherited from them" (Hood 2015).

THE CHARLESTON TRAGEDY and the political aftermath raise important questions and can serve as a springboard for a broader discussion about southern identity. Most clearly, the events show that southern identity is not merely an interesting sideshow in American discourse, but instead often plays a central role in helping us understand modern society. Revisiting the Charleston shooting raises a number of issues that we address in this chapter, particularly the role of race in the formation and maintenance of southern identity. The church shootings and their political aftermath also illustrate how southern identity can mean different things to different people. In this tragic example, Roof used his racialized southern identity to justify hatred and violence, but a different strand of southern identity was used by others as a source of strength, a way to find forgiveness, and a mechanism for enhancing community bonds.

For readers new to the topic of southern identity, it is important to note that scholars and professional observers of the South have debated, argued, and waxed poetic about the region, how southerners identify with it, and what nonsoutherners think about the South for many years. Here we highlight some of this work and show how the existing literature helps us develop the three primary questions we explore in this book.

As a first step, it is useful to place southern identity within the larger context of regional identity. There are, of course, many identifiable regions out there, both within the United States and around the globe, and many of the people living in these regions grapple with regional identity in ways that can help us understand southern identity and the South.

Next, we then turn our attention to the literature on southern identity and distinctiveness more specifically. Though our primary focus is southern identity, not southern distinctiveness, there is good evidence that distinctiveness (or at least perceived distinctiveness) is a precursor to identity. As a result, we address the issue of southern distinctiveness in this chapter by focusing on two topics near and dear to the hearts of many southerners: food and politics.

As we noted above, one of the main objectives of this book is to explore the similarities and differences in the ways blacks and whites identify with the South. To do this, we also discuss some of the existing literature that explores the complicated role of race and southern identity and attempt to disentangle the word "southerner" from any implicit connection to "white southerner." Black southerners have no doubt always considered themselves southerners, and this has only become more relevant in the decades following the civil rights movement.

As the Charleston attack reminds us, there is certainly a dark side of southern identity, an issue we also explore in this chapter. We investigate this phenomenon by looking back at some political examples, focusing particularly on the "Dixiecrat" movement, George Wallace's political rise, Nixon's "Southern Strategy," and the political use of southern symbols like the Confederate flag.

Last, it is important to grapple with the theoretical underpinnings of southern identity before embarking on our own investigation of the topic. Therefore, we borrow a few insights about social identity from sociologists and social psychologists to gain a deeper understanding of the reasons people choose to self-identify as southerners. We investigate the natural tendency for humans to self-categorize and the propensity for social comparison between in-groups and out-groups. Familiarity with the basics of social identity theory can help us better understand southern identity, provide a framework for our subsequent analyses, and give meaning to our findings in the chapters that follow.

Regional Identity

Regional identity is not a uniquely southern phenomenon. Stories about regional identification can be told around the nation and around the world (Paasi 2003). Regional identification explains why people throughout much of New England rally behind the Boston Red Sox and why members of the Basque community in Spain once cheered for the professional cycling team Euskaltel-Euskadi. Regional identity can also explain political battles, such as the fight over Quebec's independence in Canada and the divisions between the Wallonia and Flanders regions of Belgium (Ceuppens and Foblets 2008).

Given its ubiquity and importance, it is not surprising that many have tilled the soil of regional identity. Among social scientists, geographers have perhaps the longest tradition of examining region as an important construct influencing how people perceive their place in the world and how they relate to it. Most geographers have moved past static, political definitions of region and instead argue that region is best understood as a social construct exemplified by the idea of a vernacular region. Vernacular regions are "the product of the spatial perception of average people . . . neither something created by governmental, corporate, or journalistic fiat, nor the scientist's artifact, however sophisticated or otherwise, contrived to serve some specific scholarly or pedagogic purpose" (Zelinsky 1980, 1). In other words, vernacular regions are determined by average people; taken together, vernacular regions describe how people relate to the world around them.

In this work we underscore the fact that regions and regional boundaries exist regardless of the political boundaries that may officially define a place. For example, the state of Delaware sits within the U.S. Census Bureau's official definition of the South but lies decidedly outside of most people's vernacular definition of the American South. If we follow the assumption that vernacular regions are socially constructed and not necessarily exclusive, an individual may reside simultaneously in multiple vernacular regions. This is certainly true of us: we both reside in the South, but, at the same time, one of us sits in North Carolina's southern Appalachian Mountains while the other lives in South Carolina's Lowcountry.

In just one demonstration of overlapping vernacular regions, we conducted a survey of a unique area of the country—the twenty-three westernmost counties in North Carolina. What makes this area unique and important for our purposes is that residents of this area may identify as being members of multiple regions. They might call themselves "Appalachians," "North Carolinians," "Southerners," or "Americans" (Cooper and Knotts 2013). What we found, however, was that most people didn't make a choice between regional identities, but instead professed to be a member of multiple regions simultaneously.

This book, and much of our research agenda over the past decade, argues that regional identity serves a purpose. Ascribing to, or eschewing, a regional label—whether it be "Southerner," "Appalachian," "Midwesterner," "Yankee," or "Basque"—helps people make sense of their place in the social world. For some, identification with a region allows them to feel more connected to their familial roots, while for others it provides a means to connect to cultural values they associate with the region. Sociologist John Shelton Reed (1983, 11) calls regional identity the "cognitive entity that people use to orient themselves," again reinforcing that regional identity does not always overlap perfectly with actual political boundaries. He explains that "the criteria for membership in a regional group have more to do with identification than with location" (Reed 1982, 13), reflecting the notion that vernacular regions may be more useful for understanding social behavior than regions defined by states, counties, or other political borders. Because regional identification is socially constructed, the valence and intensity of an individual's regional identity may vary across her lifetime as she moves and encounters people from other places (Shortridge 1987).

Southern Identity and Distinctiveness

Although it originally began as a politically defined region, the South today has morphed into what can best be considered a vernacular region—with fuzzy (and often-debated) boundaries. Whether it is because of its political interest, its historical importance, or its unique culture, we cannot be sure, but for whatever reason, the South is the most studied region in America.[1] Perhaps the most appropriate starting place for any exposition of southern identity and distinctiveness is with W. J. Cash's monumental *The Mind of the South* ([1941] 1991). A Gaffney, South Carolina, native, and a longtime resident of North Carolina, Cash knew the South well and wrote an article called "The Mind of the South" in October 1929. After a small bit of prodding, Cash agreed to write a full-length manuscript with the same title, and, twelve years later, *The Mind of the South* was published and the attention of the country turned once again to the region. In this treatise, Cash argued that "a unified and continuous set of distinctively southern values and attitudes had not only defied but actually fed upon the upheaval of Civil War and Reconstruction and then persisted through four decades of the twentieth century despite the economic and demographic transformations accompanying urbanization and industrial expansion" (Cobb 1999, 44). Cash's southerner was defined more by continuity than change, by tradition than progress.[2]

While some, like historian C. Vann Woodward (1958), later argued that the South (and presumably southern identity) was not as static as Cash suggested, others like historian Carl Degler (1997) and John Shelton Reed (1982) agreed with Cash that southerners would always be defined, at some level, by the Civil War and Reconstruction.[3] In the words of historian John Inscoe (2011, 15), "Regional identity has long been a more integral part of southerners' self-definition than is often true elsewhere."

Sociologist Larry Griffin summarizes the sources of this collective regional identity, noting that the South was "exceptional in its fierce commitment to slavery, in its failed experiment with secession and nationhood, in its military defeat and occupation by a conquering power, in its poverty, cultural backwardness, and religiosity, and in its pervasive, prolonged resistance to racial justice." But, "just as the history of the South is contradictory and contested, so, too, is the identity of southerners" (Griffin 2006, 7).[4]

We have already established that southern identity, like regional identity more generally, is not defined solely by political or geographic boundaries, but also by personal connection. Region, therefore, must exist in the collective memory as much as it does on a map. Said differently, "if there is a South then the people who live there should recognize their kinship with one another and, by the same token, those who live outside the South ought to recognize that southerners are somehow different from them" (Degler 1997, 7–8). This recognition that southerners are somehow different is an important part of southern identity. At the same time, we want to be careful navigating between perception and reality when it comes to southern distinctiveness. Though we will cite literature and show empirical measures highlighting a continuing southern distinctiveness, there is an even stronger case to be made that people living in the region *perceive* the South to be different. Were the South not a distinct place (at least in people's minds), the taxpayers of Mississippi would likely withdraw their support from the University of Mississippi's Center for the Study of Southern Culture, Charleston South Carolina's award-winning restaurant Husk (which markets itself as offering "a celebration of southern ingredients") would not be booked weeks in advance, and the publishers of the Nuevo southern publication *Garden and Gun* would be wanting for subscribers. Whether this marks "true" distinctiveness is a much different and, at least for our purposes, a less important question.

None of this is to imply that many of the historical, cultural, psychological, and sociological processes evident in the South do not appear in other parts of the country, just that these forces have coalesced in the South to produce a region that people perceive as unique. In a conversation with a humorist and critic of the South, Chuck Thompson, Cobb summarized his view of southern distinctiveness, stating, "I never met anybody who spent any time down South who came from elsewhere in the country who didn't get a different feel from the South. I don't see that fading" (Thompson 2012, 250). We agree, and point to the considerable evidence that cultural distinctiveness remains an important component of southern identity. As we discuss in more detail in chapter 4, the best way to understand southern distinctiveness and identity may not be through traditional means, but rather through an examination of shared culture.

We borrow this emphasis on shared cultures directly from Reed (1993), who examined a range of unobtrusive measures in his quest to understand the South's cultural distinctiveness, including membership in Baptist churches, birthplaces of country music notables, and states mentioned in country music lyrics. Reed also focused on southerners' almost preternatural obsession with fireworks and guns. Although southern women are less likely than southern men to appreciate things that explode and shoot, they still prefer both guns and fireworks more than male nonsoutherners (Reed 1996). This is a case where region trumps gender. Southern language is also clearly distinct—even beyond the southern accent. Southerners are more likely to teach their children to call grown-ups "sir" and "ma'am" (Reed 1993) and more likely to refer to their mother as "mama" (Reed 1997). Southerners even feel differently about death and dying than nonsoutherners (Reed 1999). Many of these may seem like trivial distinctions, but, as we argue throughout this book, these folkways continue to define how people view the region, and their connection to it.

More recently, scholars have examined the role of kudzu in southern life, arguing that "perhaps no other part of the natural environment is more closely identified with the South than this invasive and fast-growing vine" (Alderman and Alderman 2001, 50). Among their evidence, they find that there are nineteen streets named after kudzu—and all are located in the South. Business names are no exception, as all thirty-three businesses named after the vine are located in the Census South. Following the growth of the "pernicious weed" also mirrors the growth of the South, illustrating "the tremendous impact the American South has made, and continues to make, on national culture" (Alderman and Alderman 2001, 50). As another example, social psychologist Dov Cohen used experimental methods to explore the region's culture of honor and propensity for violence. He compared the responses of southern and northern males to aggressive behavior, finding that southern males were more likely than nonsouthern males to "feel diminished" and "use aggressive or domineering behavior to reestablish his masculine status" (Cohen et al. 1996, 958). He also discovered that southerners' politeness may actually lead to violence because "conflicts bubble under the surface, only to explode later, because people do not clearly send nor clearly receive signals of anger" (Cohen et al. 1999, 273). Other examples of southern touchstones include the ever-ubiquitous sport of NASCAR, "the most southern sport on earth," which has gone national (Pierce 2001).

In sum, we argue that there are common characteristics, habits, and experiences that southerners share. This does not mean that all southerners share all of these traits (neither of us are particularly big NASCAR fans, yet we both identify as southerners), but that, taking these elements together, there remains a southern culture that provides a common set of touchstones for southerners, regardless of race, class, or gender. As the white South has evolved toward more inclusion of nonwhites, this culture has provided a way for southerners of all races to find more in common. Perhaps nowhere is this commonality more present than in southern food—a topic to which we now turn.

Food

Marcie Cohen Ferris (2009, 4) argues that "southern food is many things to many people—a vast world of meaning and symbolism and plain old eating to generations of southerners and visitors to the region." She continues by saying, "food is entangled in forces that have sharpened southern history and culture for more than four centuries. The cultural processes associated with food—production, regulation, representation, identity, and consumption—have taken on aliases such as agriculture, animal sciences, civil rights, consumption, decorative arts, domesticity, drink, economy, exchange, garden, horticulture, hunger, malnutrition, marketplace, nutrition, obesity, pottery, poverty, property, reform, segregation, slavery, starvation, sustenance, terror, trade and wealth." Food provides many shared experiences for southerners as well. Southern food is not only recognized as a commonality bringing southerners together, but is recognized by nonsoutherners as something different, something regional—something uniquely southern.

Almost without exception, southerners offer southern food as a key component of the region's distinctiveness. Take grits as an example. This culinary staple, made of ground-up corn, is probably the food most associated with the culture of the American South, and what Reed (1995, 529) calls the "national food of the South." In fact, almost half (45 percent) of people living in the South report eating grits frequently or sometimes. Of these grits eaters, about a quarter (23 percent) eat grits a few times a month or more—compared to 6 percent of nonsoutherners. Natives to the region, residents of the Deep South, self-identified southerners, rural folks, and regular churchgoers are most likely to eat grits on a regular basis. In addition, blacks and whites alike enjoy this staple of the South. In fact, grits are more popular among black southerners than white southerners, reinforcing once more that many of the commonly identified traits of southerners may apply more readily to black southerners than to white southerners.

Moving beyond grits, there are a number of other foods—okra, chitlins, pork rinds, catfish, moon pies, fried tomatoes, sweet potato pie, and boiled peanuts—traditionally associated with the South (Latshaw 2009). Comparing consumption of these foods with five foods that are rarely (if ever) included in lists of stereotypically southern foods—kielbasa, lox, arugula, venison, and caviar—uncovers some noteworthy observations.

There are large differences between the frequency with which southerners and nonsoutherners eat the most stereotypically southern foods. As our analysis of Southern Focus Poll data reveals (see table A1.1 and table A1.2), southerners are nearly four times more likely than nonsoutherners to eat okra and chitlins frequently, about three times more likely to eat boiled peanuts and moon pies, nearly twice as likely to eat catfish, and more likely to have eaten sweet potato pie and fried tomatoes. Nonsoutherners, by contrast, are much more likely to frequently eat kielbasa, and just as likely to frequently eat lox, arugula, venison, and caviar.

Clearly, food provides a key point of delineation between southerners and nonsoutherners. But, given the importance of race in the South, we were curious whether food divides or unites southern whites and blacks. In an important theme that we return to in chapter 4, we find that there are more similarities than differences in the ways black and white southerners view the region. Only sweet potato pie has a larger racial than regional division. Indeed, food seems to be an aspect of southern culture that unites, rather than divides southerners. Clearly, food provides a shared set of regional experiences for black and white southerners that is not apparent between white southerners and white nonsoutherners, or between black southerners and black nonsoutherners.

For additional evidence on the role food plays in southern distinctiveness and identity, you don't necessarily need to look toward academic studies, but simply to the popular media. In fact, author, celebrity chef, and television personality Alton Brown remarked that "southern identity doesn't exist without food" (Brown 2014, 32). Likewise, native New Yorker Bobby Flay is reportedly obsessed with the food of the South. *Food & Wine* magazine followed Flay on a trip to Savannah, Georgia, and noted that he is "a passionate advocate for the cuisine of the American South." So much so, in fact, that when he visited one of Savannah's fine-dining restaurants, and the waiter served him "a lovely seared scallop scented with vanilla, Flay joked, sotto voce, 'where are the grits?'" (Lee and Lee 2006).

Politics

Throughout most of American history, the region's political environment has also been a source of distinctiveness. In 1949, Texas native V. O. Key penned the magisterial *Southern Politics in State and Nation*—the closest thing there is to a bible of southern politics. In it, Key (1949, 5) focused on the region's political distinctiveness and argued that "in its grand outlines the politics of the South revolves around the position of the negro."

In what remains the best update to Key, Earl and Merle Black's (1987, 3) *Politics and Society in the South* argues that the major characteristics of traditional southern politics and the characteristics that made the region's politics unique were: 1) a single political party, 2) a focus on the personalities and qualifications of candidates over significant issues, 3) an environment where most adult southerners were ineligible to vote, and 4) policy outcomes tilted toward the haves over the have-nots. This era ended, of course, and the region's politics transformed based on a host of factors, including a growing middle class, urbanization, and the in-migration of people from outside the South (Black and Black 1987, 292).

There is some recent evidence, however, that the region's politics may once again be distinct. Looking across the thirteen southern states, Republican candidate Mitt Romney received 54 percent of the vote in 2012, compared to just 44 percent of the vote outside the South.[5] Moreover, Republicans currently hold 88 percent of the U.S. Senate seats from the South, compared to only 42 percent of U.S. Senate seats outside the South.[6] Republicans also have significant advantages over Democrats in U.S. House seats in the South.[7] As perhaps the most striking example of the region's political transformation, the last remaining white Democrat in Congress from the Deep South, Georgia's John Barrow, was defeated in the 2014 election (Davis 2014).

Public Opinion

Of course, election outcomes are just one measure of the region's political landscape. In the 1950s, southerners, and in many cases younger southerners, had more conservative opinions than nonsoutherners on a host of issues, including morality, politics, religion, international relations, and, of course, race (Glenn and Simmons 1967). Reed's (1972) early work focused on religiosity, a tolerance for violence, and a propensity for localism as hall-marks of southern distinctiveness. Summarizing much of this work, Jeanne Hurlbert (1989, 251) identified three dimensions of southern distinctive-ness between 1972 and 1982: attitudes on racial and women's issues, religious/moral attitudes, and attitudes on politics and individual freedom. A more recent study demonstrated that southerners exhibited more conservative at-titudes on issues including race, gender, religion, sex, and tolerance (Rice, McLean, and Larson 2002).

Is public opinion in the South still distinctive? To find out, we analyzed survey responses from the 2012 American National Election Study (ANES). The folks at the ANES asked respondents living in the South and non-South how they felt about twenty-nine groups on a scale of 0–100, where 100 indi-cates that the person feels "warm" towards that group and a 0 indicates they feel "cold" (American National Election Study 2012). Our complete results are available in table A1.3.

As you might expect, respondents living in the South reported warmer feelings (relative to respondents living outside the South) about Christian Fundamentalists, Christians, Big Business, the Military, the Federal Gov-ernment, People on Welfare, Poor People, Congress, Blacks, Conservatives, the U.S. Supreme Court, Rich People, Illegal Immigrants, the Democratic Party, Hispanics, and Working Class People. Relative to geographic non-southerners, geographic southerners were much cooler toward Muslims, Catholics, Gay Men and Lesbians and Atheists. But, it is also important to note that there were *not* meaningful differences in opinion on 30 percent of the issues and groups listed in table A1.3.

Why the Differences Make a Difference

While some readers may dismiss these explications of southern distinctive-ness on culture, food, politics, and public opinion as frivolous explana-tions of the obvious, we believe when put together, they reveal something more subtle and important. Recall Degler's (1997, 7–8) statement that "if there is a South then the people who live there should recognize their kin-ship with one another and, by the same token, those who live outside the South ought to recognize that southerners are somehow different from them." We believe that there is a southern "otherness," and this is re-flected in the region's culture, food, politics, and public opinion, among other things.[8]

The standard social science retort to our argument would be to suggest that these differences are not due to region at all, but rather to race, class, politics, climate, geography, or a host of other factors that just happen to take place in the South. According to this argument, there is nothing special about the South per se—it's just a holding area for folks of a certain demographic makeup. And if you were to place those same people in New Jersey, you'd find the same trends we identify above.

This argument may be appealing for those concerned with the causes of differences, but it is less important for our purposes. The fact is, this collection of people did develop in the South. And these people developed cultural norms and political attitudes that affected their behavior, and ultimately influenced politics and culture in the United States writ large. In the same way that social scientists often talk about "path dependence" (the notion that our actions today are affected by our actions in the past, even if the conditions that precipitated the original action have disappeared), southern distinctiveness continues today. And, these differences exist in people's minds as well. There is perhaps no better example of this than the lingering effects of slavery. As Acharya, Blackwell, and Sen (2016) explain, blacks who live in places that once held higher densities of slaves today experience demonstrably worse race relations and higher levels of overt discrimination than blacks who live in other locations in the South. This is not a historical accident, but rather is due to the behavioral path dependence of racism and white supremacy that is passed down from generation to generation in these enclaves of white rule.

One group of scholars even holds that southerners (or, more specifically white southerners) can be considered an ethnic group (Reed 1973; Tindall 1976), "serving the same functions for its members and related to the American majority in much the same way as groups more conventionally considered 'ethnic,' such as Irish-, Polish-, or Lithuanian-Americans" (Reed 1973, 233). Through both force of argument and a relentless accumulation of data, Reed contends that white southerners share both historical circumstances and the "sense of peoplehood" that emanates from that history—thus making them, in essence, an ethnic group, or at least a "quasi-ethnic group" (Reed 1993, 41).

When considered as an analogy rather than an explicit description (Reed 1973, 240), the notion of southerners as an ethnic group can provide a framework for understanding what unites white southerners. Taken literally, however, this description is unnecessarily exclusionary. Southerners simply are not united around a common language, nationality, or culture in the same way as traditional ethnic groups. Further, Reed's and Tindall's focus on white southerners diminishes the power of the concept of regional identity as a true uniting force, and excludes over a quarter of the region's population.

A more productive approach to southern identity is to determine the similarities and differences between how southerners of a variety of races and religions connect to the region. This is even more necessary as "the demise of Jim Crow has created both the opportunity and the increasing desire of black southerners to assert their own identity as southerners" (Thompson and Sloan 2012, 73). A complete understanding of the South and of southern identity must therefore embrace southern cultures, rather than forcing all southerners into a single, monolithic southern culture.[9]

Race and Southern Identity

Race is, of course, vital to understanding the causes, prevalence, and consequences of southern identity. For much of southern history, when someone talked about "southerners," they were generally referring to "white southerners." And for much of this history, white southerners were united around maintaining the racial order. "The movement to reform the late Old South into an ideal, unitary order of masters and slaves, whites and blacks, was a drive to achieve what might be called an 'organic' society. In that order there would be various parts in the social body, and every party would have its place and function" (Williamson 1984, 24). Striking a similar tone, Ulrich B. Phillips (1928, 31) argued that this commitment to preserving the racial order, what he called "a white man's country," was "the cardinal test of a Southerner and the central theme of Southern history."

Race has certainly been a wedge issue in the region, frequently used to form, unify, and maintain a particular type of southern identity. It is, of course, not surprising that much of the ugly racial history and animosity in the region emanates from the legacy of slavery (Acharya, Blackwell, and Sen 2016), and, as we previously mentioned, southern whites "made racial supremacy the cornerstone of their regional identity" and "it also became the cornerstone of their resistance to northern intrusions in general" (Cobb 2005a, 3). The traditional role of racism in southern identity also excluded African Americans, a group that made up a substantial proportion of the southern population. As Cobb (2005a, 5) notes, "the definition of southern identity effectively excluded the South's black residents in much the same way that both black and white southerners had been 'othered' out of the construction of American identity." Rhetorician Rebecca Bridges Watts (2008, 3–4) levies a similar criticism, noting that "in common parlance, Southerners often refers to white southerners—specifically, those white southerners who proudly identify themselves as such."

Despite some obvious differences, it is increasingly clear that black and white southerners today do share regional identity in common. In the words of David Goldfield (2002, 284), "blacks have inhabited the region for generations, longer than most whites, and their ancestors remain in the soil of the South. Migration elsewhere did not dim their love for the region, even as southern whites did their best to make it otherwise." In his 1979 book, *Journeys Through the South: A Rediscovery*, former *New York Times* reporter Fred Powledge noted that "black people *are* Southerners. They are of and by and from and for the South at least as much as their white brethren, and many have repeatedly demonstrated . . . their love for and faith in the region" (quoted in Cobb 2005a, 264). In a similar vein, political scientist Robert Mickey (2015, xiii) argues that "viewing 'southerners' as meaning only 'whites' writes blacks out of a region they helped forge. . . . Blacks are southerners, too."

In a particularly trenchant account of the ways blacks and whites identify with the South, two sociologists interviewed thirty-two black and thirty-three white southerners between 2004 and 2005 and found that both blacks and whites "emphasized the positive aspects of the region and disassociated themselves from the negative views" (Thompson and Sloan 2012, 77). The key difference between black and white participants was that half of the African Americans talked about race when asked about southern identity but none of the whites mentioned race when asked about the same topic. The authors concluded that "for many African Americans, black history is southern history, and southern history is black history—and for our black southern respondents, both of these histories, regional and racial, take on personal significance" (83).

Today, as the demographic profile of the region expands, we could make many of the same arguments about Hispanics in the South. An analysis of demographic trends of Latinos in the South even led Lamare et al. (2012, 213) to proclaim, "Fajitas are not as prevalent on southern menus as chicken fried steak. Yet." In fact, eight of the nine states with the fastest-growing Latino populations between 2000 and 2010 were located in the Census South (Ennis, Rios-Vargas, and Albert 2011). Though we focus on the opinions of blacks and whites in this book, it is clear to us that future treatments of southern identity should also address the region's increasing ethnic diversity—focusing specifically on the ways in which Latinos, Native Americans and geographic southerners of all racial and ethnic groups adopt or eschew southern identity. We return to this point more explicitly in the conclusion.

The Dark Side of Southern Identity

As we noted above, southern identity has been used, and misused, by politicians and social movements to advance a populist and often racist political agenda. This misuse of southern identity has allowed white supremacist attitudes to be conflated with other forms of southern identity in many people's minds, and has continued to perpetuate the "dark side of southern identity."[10]

Following President Harry Truman's support for civil rights legislation in 1948, southern Democratic leaders formed the States' Rights Democratic Party, also known as the Dixiecrats, and selected South Carolina governor Strom Thurmond to be its leader (Frederickson 2001). The formation of the Dixiecrats represents a noteworthy instance of appealing to southern pride to oppress racial minorities and defend what political demagogues referred to as "the southern way of life" (Bass and Thompson 1998). Appealing to this sense of regional pride, Thurmond declared that "there's not enough troops in the Army to force the Southern people to break down segregation and admit the nigger race into our theaters, into our swimming pools, into our homes, and into our churches" (Crespino 2012, 71).

At the same time as Thurmond was railing against integration, Confederate flag sales increased markedly. In fact, a Dallas store reported a "three thousand percent increase" in sales following the 1948 Dixiecrat convention, and a Richmond store estimated the increase at "10 thousand percent" (Coski 2005, 105).[11] It is difficult to deny that the timing of the increase fell almost in lockstep with the Dixiecrat campaign.

Another glaring example of the dark side of southern identity can be seen in the actions of four-term Alabama governor George C. Wallace. Wallace fueled the flames of racial discrimination to gain political power and had a particularly strong appeal to southern whites (Carter 1995). In his 1963 inaugural address as Alabama governor, Wallace made outright appeals to southern history, southern heritage, and southern culture. He spoke defiantly from the steps of the Alabama State Capitol in Montgomery, noting that

It is very appropriate that from this cradle of Confederacy, this very heart of the great Angle-Saxon Southland, that today we sound the drum of freedom as have our generations of forebears before us time and again through history. Let us rise to the call for freedom-loving blood that is in us and send our answer to the tyranny that clanks its chains upon the South. In the name of the greatest people that have ever trod this earth, I draw a line in the dust and toss the gauntlet before the feet of tyranny, and I say segregation now, segregation tomorrow, segregation forever. (Wallace 1963)

Capitalizing on civil unrest and continued racial strife, Wallace mounted a third-party presidential run in 1968, garnering nearly 10 million votes and winning five southern states.

The dark side of southern identity can also be seen in the Republican Party's "Southern Strategy," a targeted effort to appeal to white southerners' dissatisfaction with the racial and welfare policies of the national Democratic Party (Phillips 1969). Presidential candidate Barry Goldwater made direct appeals to southern whites in 1964, referencing states' rights, tax cuts, and federal intervention in civil rights, but the Republican's "Southern Strategy" was most evident in the 1972 election between Richard Nixon and George McGovern. Others have even pointed to the political rise of Ronald Reagan as an example of how politicians use racial wedge issues to gain support from white voters in the South. According to Juan Williams (2004),

After he defeated President Carter, a native Southerner, Reagan led an administration that seemed to cater to Southerners still angry over the passage of the Civil Rights Act after 16 years. The Reagan team condemned busing for school integration, opposed affirmative action and even threatened to veto a proposed extension of the Voting Rights Act (the sequel to the 1964 Civil Rights Act passed a year later and focused on election participation). President Reagan also tried to allow Bob Jones University, a segregated Southern school, to reclaim federal tax credits that had long been denied to racially discriminatory institutions. (n.p.)

In perhaps the most explicit admission of the ways politicians used race in the southern strategy, notorious Republican strategist (and South Carolina native) Lee Atwater summarized the approach: "You start out in 1954 by saying, 'Nigger, nigger, nigger.' By 1968 you can't say 'nigger'—that hurts you, backfires. So you say stuff like, uh, forced busing, states' rights, and all that stuff, and you're getting so abstract. Now, you're talking about cutting taxes, and all these things you're talking about are totally economic things and a byproduct of them is, blacks get hurt worse than whites" (Lamis 1999, 8).

Former Republican National Committee chairman Ken Mehlman even issued an apology for the southern strategy in a 2005 speech, noting that "Some Republicans gave up on winning the African American vote, looking the other way or trying to benefit politically from racial polarization. I am here today as the Republican chairman to tell you we were wrong" (Allen 2005).

Although the dark side of southern identity has become less direct and more coded, it continues to be used to gain and maintain political power. A team of social psychologists provided further support for this argument by demonstrating that when people were primed with pictures of the Confederate flag (presumably a call to the "dark side of southern identity"), their support for Barack Obama declined. In a separate experiment, they showed that exposing people to the Confederate flag also produced diminished levels of support for a hypothetical black candidate, but their levels of support for a white candidate remained constant (Ehrlinger et al. 2011). Clearly, symbols of the Old South are still pervasive; politicians and leaders who appeal to southern identity should be wary of these polarizing consequences.

The Social Psychology of Southern Identity

Scholars have identified three potential reasons someone might identify with the South, noting that "folks will more likely think of themselves as southerners if they have a consciousness of the South as distinctive, perceive it in stereotypically positive ways (and spurn negative stereotypes), and identify with and believe themselves similar to others in the region and dissimilar from regional outsiders" (Griffin 2006, 12).

Cobb has also written about the formation of southern identity by building on Susan-Mary Grant's assertion that southerners serve as a "negative reference point" for people living outside the region (Cobb 2005a, 3). In Cobb's view, southern identity emerges as much from a sense of what the South is not, as what it is. If American identity was defined by urbanization, industrialization, and ethnic diversity, many white southerners united behind the antithesis of these ideas (Degler 1997).

When it comes to developing a theory of southern identity, however, Cobb (2005a, 6) proceeds with considerable caution, saying that years of research on identity theory has left him "bleary eyed, brain befogged, and not much the wiser for it all." But, he does advance important elements about southern identity that we adopt and augment in the chapters that follow. Cobb's vision of southern identity begins with a contrast between North and South. While comparisons to the North remain a key part of southern identity, perhaps the most important component of Cobb's perspective is how it accounts for change. "The experience of the South affords proof enough that identity is not a fixed and immutable condition, but as Lawrence Levine suggests of culture, an ongoing interactive 'process' in which adaptability, rather than resistance, to change is more often than not the real key to survival" (7).

Another promising approach has been to ground southern identity research within the literature on social identity, defined as "the individual's knowledge that he [or she] belongs to certain social groups together with some emotional and value significance to him of this group membership" (Tajfel 1972, 292, cited in Hogg 2006). Reed (1983, 7–10) himself drew upon the work of social psychology pioneer Kurt Lewin as the "theoretical underpinnings" for his book *Southerners: The Social Psychology of Sectionalism*, noting that "Lewin's concern, and mine, is with the individual's 'life space' (his cognitive field or psychological environment), that is, with his environment *as he sees it* and with the properties and relations of entities within it." Likewise, Griffin (2006, 8) argued that the decision to identify as a southerner "is a function of choices they make—choices, however, constrained by biography, perception of the region and its inhabitants, and social interactions, with some southerners arguably having the greater latitude in their self-definitions than others."

Social groups, defined as "a set of individuals who hold a common social identification or view themselves as members of some social category" (Stets and Burke 2000, 225), are also important to social identity theory. As you might expect, this line of research makes a further distinction between in-groups and out-groups, or the "us" versus "them." For our purposes, southerners are the in-group, and nonsoutherners are the out-group.

In addition, there are two noteworthy factors in social identity formation—self-categorization and social comparison (Stets and Burke 2000). This perspective is strikingly similar to research on partisan identification (the choice to affiliate as a Democrat or Republican), which points to the importance of affinity and self-categorization to the formation of group identity and the fact that members of social groups "tend to view the group and its member in a positive light" (Green, Palmquist, and Schickler

2002, 25). The result of self-categorization is "an accentuation of the perceived similarities between the self and other in-group members, and an accentuation of the perceived differences between the self and out-group members." Conversely, social comparison results in "the selective application of the accentuation effect, primarily to those dimensions that will result in self-enhancing outcomes for the self. Specifically, one's self-esteem is enhanced by evaluating the in-group and the out-group on dimensions that lead the in-group to be judged positively and the out-group to be judged negatively" (Stets and Burke 2000, 225). Both Reed (1983) and Griffin (2006) have shown that southerners self-categorize and make social comparisons to nonsoutherners. We build on these arguments in the pages that follow.

Reed also provides a useful way to think about the choices inherent in adopting or eschewing southern identity by highlighting two important groups. "Assimilated southerners" are individuals who move to the region and then subsequently begin to think of themselves as southerners (Reed 1983). "Lapsed southerners," on the other hand, have lived in the South all of their lives but do not identify with the region.

Griffin (2006) expands on these concepts and uses survey data to gain a sense of how likely people living in the South are to assimilate or lapse. He finds that 51 percent of migrants to the region identify as southerners, providing tangible evidence that quite a bit of assimilation is taking place. The likelihood that an individual will lapse is much lower. Using the same data, Griffin finds that only 7 percent of individuals who have lived in the South their entire life do not identify as southerners. He also identifies characteristics that make a person more likely to assimilate, discovering that "migrants to the region who feel close to other southerners are two and a half times more likely to identify as southern—that is, to assimilate—than those who lack such closeness." Moreover, he concludes that "lifelong southerners lapse almost four times more frequently if they believe two or three negative stereotypes about southerners than if they accept none or only one" (22).

Summing Up

This chapter offers a few key takeaways. First, regional identity provides a useful lens to help people locate their geographic, cultural, and social psychological place in a vast and rapidly changing world. This is true across the globe and, most importantly for our purposes, in the American South. Second, southern identity and distinctiveness have a long, frequently studied, and controversial past. Southern identity was once primarily associated (at least in the scholarly mind, if not the mind of actual southerners) almost exclusively with white southerners, but today there is evidence that black southerners are as likely as whites to consider themselves southerners. And third, because identity is in part a social psychological, rather than an exclusively geographic or political construct, people may opt in or out of southern identity, regardless of their physical location. Moving to the South may cause someone to adopt the southerner label, just as leaving it may lead a person to eschew it (although many choose to keep it despite leaving the physical geography of the South). Interactions with southerners or non-southerners may elicit the same response. In short, group identity serves a basic human need for self-categorization and social comparison and helps people find their place in the world.

While these takeaways are important, this brief foray into southern identity also leaves us with a number of unsolved puzzles that we investigate in the upcoming chapters. As we noted in the introduction, our study is focused on three primary research questions. First, how typical is southern identity today? Much has changed in the world, but we need a better sense of the magnitude of southern identity in the twenty-first century. Second, what types of people are most likely to identify as southerners? This is an important question because we know surprisingly little about the types of people who do (and do not) identify with the region. Specifically, few studies examine the question of southern identity using techniques that allow researchers to compare the relative importance of a number of potential explanations for a particular outcome. For instance, we know that a slightly higher percentage of blacks than whites identify as southerners. But, one possible explanation to this finding is that blacks are more likely to have lived in the South all of their lives than are whites. Without fully investigating these alternative explanations, we simply cannot determine whether race, time in the region, both, or neither, can explain southern identity. Third, why do people from diverse backgrounds, particularly diverse racial backgrounds, identity with the South? Aside from the recent qualitative work by Thompson and Sloan (2012), we know very little about *why* southerners connect with the region. We now turn our attention to these questions, beginning with our analysis of place naming in chapter 2.

CHAPTER TWO

Signs of the South

For most folks, the name Dixie State College probably conjures up images of an educational experience from a prior century, and one almost certainly located far south of the Mason-Dixon Line. Dixie State, however, isn't a historical artifact and isn't located in the Deep South. It is a modern four-year campus located in St. George, Utah—smack in the middle of Mormon country.[1]

The area folklore suggests that it was Mormon leader Brigham Young who once coined this area of the country "Utah's Dixie," because of its warm climate and fertile land that was thought to be suitable for growing cotton. Many historians claim, however, that the name is not so benign, citing evidence that the area was home to many Confederate sympathizers. According to Utah historian Will Bagley, "the name Dixie reflects the sympathy that the southern Utah and the Mormon people felt for the Confederacy" (quoted in Maffly 2012).

Although the Dixie State College name did not invoke much protest in its early years, the name came under more scrutiny when coupled with a number of the school's institutions and practices that many felt were racially insensitive. These included statues venerating Confederate war heroes, the prominent display of the Confederate flag, a yearbook named "The Confederate," dorms named for plantations, and an administration that was accused of turning a blind eye to students who dressed in blackface for Halloween (Whitehurst 2013a, 2013b). While some argued these were isolated incidents and examples taken out of context, others believed that they reflected a college that was unconcerned with the potential negative consequences of the symbols they had chosen. As an NAACP leader noted, "They must not want any people of color to go to that university" (Whitehurst 2013b).

When the mission of Dixie State became more consistent with that of a full-scale university than a small college, the school's leadership decided to explore a name change. It was a foregone conclusion that they abandon the "College" moniker and become known as a "University," but there was considerably more debate about whether to keep "Dixie" as part of its name. Those opposing the name change appealed to tradition and denied that the name carried with it any implicit connotations of racial discrimination.

"I can tell you that no one who lives there that's worked to make this happen has any thought of discrimination or bigotry or any such thing," said a state representative from St. George (Grimmett 2013). Those supporting a name change made their case in a change.org (2013) petition stating, "It is time to cut all ties with the identity of the Confederate South to promote and support diversity on campus."

With the position of each side firmly staked out, Dixie State hired a consulting firm to perform a market analysis and develop a solution to satisfy both camps. The firm concluded that the college should keep the Dixie name if it wanted to maintain its local focus, whereas a regional or national orientation would best be served by a change that eliminated Dixie from the school's name (Sorenson 2013).

In February 2013, the university's Board of Trustees voted to keep the Dixie moniker, adopting the formal name Dixie State University. According to the Board chairman, Steven Caplin, "We unanimously stand behind the Dixie State University name . . . no one on this board or in this administration is aware of any racial discrimination in our past" (Whitehurst 2013b).

THOUGH DIXIE STATE UNIVERSITY is located more than five hundred miles away from even the most generous definition of the geographic South, the naming controversy there provides a number of important lessons that guide our understanding of southern identity more broadly. First, it reinforces the idea that regional identity is not entirely defined by formal political boundaries but owes at least as much to how people perceive themselves and their place in the world. As Reed (1976, 934) once noted, the word Dixie "has more to do with attitude than latitude." Despite the somewhat northerly latitude, there is still considerable southern attitude in a university that prints a yearbook named "The Confederate" and celebrates a rebel mascot.

Second, this story illustrates that names carry with them powerful meanings that may change over time. Those who rallied against the Dixie name were concerned that maintaining the status quo would lead to lower minority enrollments, less grant-funding, and a university that would never attain national prominence. For those who wanted to keep the Dixie name, however, the name was associated with respect for tradition and place. Similar debates can be seen throughout the South, as southerners struggle with how to simultaneously venerate what they view as the positive aspects of the region while avoiding its negative pitfalls.

Third, the meaning assigned to a particular place varies based on a person's background and experience. Older members of the Dixie State community often felt a stronger connection to the name than newer faculty and staff (Sorensen 2013). Anecdotal evidence also suggests that groups and people concerned with minority rights, like the NAACP, were less likely to view the name as benign. Similar patterns can be seen throughout debates over southern identity; people who choose to identify with the South are systematically different on a number of factors than their counterparts who eschew the label.

Fourth, selecting a name (as the college founders did in 1916) and keeping a name, (as the university opted to do in 2013) is a conscious choice. College leaders could have eliminated or altered the Dixie name at any point in the school's history, but did not. Keeping the name Dixie State tells us a lot about the college's values and how its leaders wish it to be perceived. Similarly, other regional names and their retention inform us about how leaders of these institutions view their place in the world.

Fifth, people who identify with one place or institution (in this case, the college) may do so for different reasons and may view that identification in different ways. Both sides in the Dixie State controversy claimed to identify, care for, and even love the institution, but they also disagreed vehemently about what that identity suggests for the future. We see this lesson demonstrated time and time again across the South.

In this chapter, we use the example of Dixie State and the lessons it teaches us to jump-start a broader investigation of place naming as a way to understand southern identity today. One of our primary questions is, just how typical is southern identity today, particularly in light of the dramatic political and social changes that have occurred in the region? As an initial strategy, we investigate business names as one measure of southern identification. Using this measure, we show that southern identity remains quite strong. However, we also use the same evidence to demonstrate that the nature of southern identity has changed rather dramatically.

What's in a Name?

The strategy of studying naming as a window into identity may seem a bit unorthodox. As the Dixie State story demonstrates, however, place naming gives us a number of important signals about how people conceive of themselves and their relationship to place. "Naming is a noteworthy cultural practice not only because of its ability to create a sense of continuity over time but also through its capacity for changing and challenging lines of identity" (Alderman 2008, 195).

In contrast to formal delineations of region that appear on a map or are provided by an official agency like the Census Bureau, place names, or toponyms, are also important because they give us a sense of the "vernacular region." As we discussed in chapter 1, vernacular regions reflect how regular people talk about place, and studying them can give us important insights into the nature of identity today.

Examining toponyms, therefore, can give us clues about broader societal trends and tell us more about changing identity as according to Berg and Kearns (1996, 99), place naming "involves a contested identity politics of people and place" and addresses issues related to "the social construction of space and the symbolic construction of meanings about place." In contrast to surveys and experiments, the analysis of place naming is not invasive and is not susceptible to many of the human biases that haunt other methods of data collection. Place names don't lie, they don't deceive, and they don't give answers that are socially desirable. Place names are, to borrow a phrase from social psychologist Sam Gosling (2008), a type of "behavioral residue," and represent one of the clues people and societies leave behind—clues that can help uncover the mystery of who they are and how they perceive their place in the world.

Research on naming occupies a comparatively small place in the scholarly literature, but that does not imply that it is an unimportant one. Indeed, an intrepid group of scholars have learned a great deal about culture and geography by investigating place names in a variety of areas. As mentioned in chapter 1, there has been work on streets and businesses with the word "kudzu" in them (Alderman and Alderman 2001), a considerable literature about the decision to name a street after Martin Luther King Jr. and its economic impacts (Alderman 2006; Light 2004; Mitchelson, Alderman, and Popke 2007; Rose-Redwood 2008), research on civil rights memorials (Dwyer and Alderman 2008), and even studies on the patriotic significance of county names (Zelinsky 1988). Because of our focus on southern identity, we review and then build on the literature on business names in the American South to gain a better understanding about the current state of southern identity and how it has evolved over the past half century.

Business Names in the South

In the 1970s, John Shelton Reed combed phone books from a "vaguely purposive" (Reed 1976, 926) collection of cities for all business names beginning with the words "Dixie," "Southern," or "American." He argued that

"Dixie" businesses were signs of the Old South, and "Southern" businesses signified the presence of the New South. The number of American entries, as we explain below, was never meant to be substantively important, but was instead collected to account for the population in each city. By counting the frequency of all three types of businesses and doing some simple division, Reed argued that resulting proportions could tell us a great deal about the prevalence and nature of southern identity.

Reed is not alone in thinking that this Old South versus New South distinction represents a key historical tension in southern identity. Celebration of the Old South has long been tied to the American Civil War and its aftermath. Communities erected monuments, renamed roads, and constructed schools in tribute to fallen soldiers, military leaders, and other embodiments of the "Lost Cause." For some, the Old South even evoked "images of kindly old master with his mint julep, happy darkies singing in the fields, coquettish belles wooed by slender gallants" (Tindall 1989, 1097).

Though ties to the Old South were strong, shortly after the Civil War regional boosters soon began promoting a New South, where "economic regeneration was the region's most pressing need" (Mixon 1989, 1113). Henry W. Grady, *Atlanta Constitution* publisher and New South advocate, described a region with "a hundred farms for every plantation, fifty homes for every palace, and a diversified industry that meets the complex needs of this complex age" (Grady 1886).

Both Old South and New South mythical images continued during the twentieth century. The Old South was most famously depicted in Margaret Mitchell's 1936 Pulitzer Prize–winning book, *Gone with the Wind*, and the 1939 Oscar-winning movie adaptation. In the political realm, "states' rights" was the rallying cry for Dixiecrat presidential candidate Strom Thurmond and the widespread opposition to racial integration and political rights for African Americans in the region (Crespino 2012). Just as they had nearly a century before, New South advocates emerged to portray a forward-looking, economically vital region. Following the desegregation of four Atlanta high schools, the region's self-appointed capital began to tout itself as "the city too busy to hate" (Hein 1972). New South boosters promoted a business-friendly climate and helped encourage state and local governments to promote the region's economic transformation by incentivizing businesses to move to the South (Mixon 1989). By the 1970s, some began to refer to the region as the "Sunbelt South," a region known for a "casual and inviting lifestyle, a favorable business climate, and conservative politics increasingly inclined to Republicanism" (Bernard 1989, 732).

These changes brought considerable growth to the South but they also coincided with a dramatic movement of whites from the region's central cities to metropolitan suburbs. This demographic shift perpetuated racial segregation and, as some have argued, gave birth to the modern conservative movement (Kruse 2007; Lassiter 2007).

In an effort to explore this Old South–New South distinction in more detail, Reed created two measures, which he called "D scores" and "S scores." Originally, he published this work in 1976 and, along with two collaborators, published an update of his findings in 1990. In both studies, D scores were calculated by dividing the number of "Dixie" entries in a city by the number of "American" entries in a city. In contrast, S scores represented a ratio of the number of "Southern" businesses to the number of "American" businesses. For example, if City A had 50 "Dixie" businesses, 100 "American" businesses, and 100 "Southern" businesses, it would receive a D score of .5 (50/100) and an S score of 1.0 (100/100). Alternatively, if City B had 25 "Dixie" businesses, 100 "American" businesses, and 90 "Southern" businesses, it would garner a D score of .25 (25/100) and an S score of .9 (90/100).

In his 1976 study, Reed found that mapping both "Southern" and "Dixie" businesses provided instructive measures of southern identity. "Southern" businesses were generally better represented than "Dixie" businesses (the average S score was higher than the average D score), but both measures were highest in the Deep South and decreased fairly consistently the farther one departed from traditional definitions of the region.

According to Reed's analysis, all of Alabama and Mississippi and nearly all of Georgia, South Carolina, and Tennessee appeared in the highest D score category. The exceptions were metropolitan Atlanta and Charlotte as well as portions of Eastern Tennessee and Western North Carolina. While the first two exceptions probably stemmed from the large number of in-migrants located in these metropolitan centers, the East Tennessee/Western North Carolina deviation has roots back to the Civil War, when these areas were marked by a number of union strongholds. Several other states were split between this highest category and the middle category (.15 to .25), including Arkansas, Kentucky, Louisiana, North Carolina, and portions of Florida. The lowest category (.06 to .15) ran through a number of peripheral South states and even extended into small portions of Illinois, Maryland, Missouri, Ohio, and West Virginia.

Reed also mapped S scores in his 1976 study, highlighting two notable differences with D scores. First, S scores were, on average, higher than D scores. Simply put, there were a lot more "Southern" businesses than "Dixie" businesses. This provided some indication of the prevalence of the "New South" over the "Old South." Second, the highest category (.60 and higher) incorporated nearly all of Louisiana and North Carolina, indicating that the "New South" had a larger geographic spread.

Fortunately this line of research allows us to see how definitions of the region have changed over the past several decades, giving us the opportunity to address our first question about the resilience of southern identity. In fact, there have been several replications of Reed's original 1976 study. The first update came from Reed, Kohls, and Hanchette (1990) and relied on business names collected in the late 1980s. They discovered that the prevalence of "Southern" businesses remained fairly constant, although the boundaries of the region shifted, using this definition. Conversely, "Dixie" businesses had experienced considerable erosion between 1976 and 1988 (222).

Using these two seminal studies as a springboard, geographers Derek Alderman and Robert Maxwell Beavers (1999) once again collected business names—this time in 1998. Even more important than what their data revealed, however, was the framework they provided to understand these changes. They suggested that the dramatic decline in "Dixie" businesses was a result of the larger phenomenon of "de-Confederatization." A high-profile example of "de-Confederatization" is the University of Mississippi abandoning its "Colonel Reb" mascot in favor of the Black Bear. While organizations like the Sons of Confederate Veterans opposed these modifications, the NAACP, among other groups, has supported these changes, arguing that "the romanticism around the Old South is 'a view of history that ignores how racism became a tool to maintain a system of supremacy and dominance'" (Weissert 2011).

The second component of their framework was re-Confederatization, a concept employed as a likely response to de-Confederatization. Re-Confederatization represents an increase in place names honoring the Old South, and was driven almost exclusively by white southerners. The Sons of Confederate Veterans' recent successful appeal to create license plates in Georgia featuring the Confederate flag is a notable, but not rare, example of this trend (Chasmar 2014).

With Reed's data collection strategy and Alderman and Beavers's conceptual framework as our guide, we conducted work on naming over three decades after Reed's initial study (see Cooper and Knotts 2010a).[2] We investigated the now familiar list of 100 "vaguely purposive" cities and discovered that the average D score dropped to .05, and the highest category

(D > .25) only appeared in southern Alabama and southern Mississippi. These findings were much different than those from Reed's 1976 work, where all of Alabama and Mississippi, and nearly all of Georgia, South Carolina, and Tennessee were in the highest D score category. When looking at our 2010 D score map, "de-Confederatization" continued to be the dominant trend in the region. Research conducted at about the same time confirms this decline in "Dixie"—so much so, in fact, that one author refers to "Dixie Islands" to represent the sporadic and geographically isolated concentration of "Dixie" businesses (Ambinakudige 2009).

A much different picture emerges when we investigated S scores. We discovered that the mean S score in 2008 was .35, and a large portion of the South remained in the highest S score category (S > .6). It is worth noting that our S score maps looked quite similar to Reed's (1976) original S score maps, despite being created over three decades apart. Given the continued stability of S scores and the fact that S scores even increased in some cities, we labeled this phenomenon "re-southernization." We believe this concept of "re-southernization" can help explain how the geographic southerners continue to express southern identity, while simultaneously trying to distance themselves from parts of the Old South past.

Looking back at this line of research, we have learned a great deal about the boundaries of the South, the state of southern identification, and changes in southern identification over time. The South remains an identifiable area, but the level of identity varies across the region. We suspected that southern identity was much stronger in Alabama and Mississippi than in Florida, Texas, or even Virginia, and the historical evidence on business naming confirms this suspicion. This research also demonstrates that identity can be expressed in different ways. The decision to include "Dixie" in the name of a business is likely different than deciding to include the word "Southern," and we suspect that the dynamics around these decisions say a lot about changing regional identity.

There is still much we do not know about these patterns of naming, however. First, we do not know whether these results hold outside of Reed's original sample of cities. As you may remember, Reed relied on a "vaguely purposive" sample of cities—some inside the South and some outside the South—some big, some small. Though we replicated his strategy in our initial work, we concede that this procedure certainly produces some odd choices. Wilmington, a fairly sizeable city on North Carolina's coast, is not included, but Asheville, a comparably sized city in the North Carolina mountains, is included. In addition, decidedly nonsouthern locales, like Duluth, Minnesota, and Des Moines, Iowa, were part of Reed's sample and might skew the overall averages cited above. In sum, before we can hang our hat on these results, we need to know whether they still hold when using a more systematic and defensible sample of cities.

Just as importantly, we do not know anything about the characteristics of the businesses named "Dixie" and whether they differ from the types of businesses named "Southern." Reed called "Dixie" a "purer measure," noting that "a business or organization may use Southern in its name simply as descriptive term, but Dixie is less likely to be used that way." In Reed's view, "The dual nature of Southern and the less ambiguous connotations of Dixie mean that while Southern can be substituted for Dixie, in general, the converse is not always true" (1976, 933). As we think about this line of research, we would expect that businesses named "Dixie" might be smaller, older, and more likely to represent blue-collar and "old economy" sectors, but this assertion has not been tested.

Finally, we have no evidence (systematic or otherwise) from business owners themselves. Why did they choose the names they chose? Would they choose them again? Do they think their names represent the South? And if so, which South?

Moving Forward

To gain a more complete understanding of the puzzle of southern identity today, we analyzed a host of previously unexplored evidence on naming. First, we created a more systematic tally of "Dixie" and "Southern" businesses in all cities with populations of 50,000 or above. In total, we collected information on 218 cities across thirteen states (the eleven states of the Confederacy plus Kentucky and Oklahoma). As we noted above, Reed relied on a "vaguely purposive" sample of cities. Further, Reed only included businesses that began with the words "Dixie" or "Southern," ignoring businesses where the key words appear elsewhere in the name of the business. This procedure was certainly defensible in the days of paper telephone books, but it unnecessarily ignores a number of businesses, such as the coyly named "Two Chicks from Dixie" gift shop in Jackson, Mississippi. Excluding these businesses might give an incomplete picture of the presence (or absence) of southern identity today. As a result, we collected our business names from a much larger group of cities and included business names with our key words "Dixie," "Southern," or "American" anywhere in the name.

Apart from these two deviations, we were as faithful as possible to Reed's original investigation—including eliminating the Winn Dixie chain of grocery stores from our analysis. As Reed found, Winn Dixie stores are not evenly distributed across the region and have their largest presence in Florida. In fact, including the grocery chain in our tally would make Florida appear as the most southern state in the country. While neither of us are native Floridians, we've spent enough time in the Sunshine State to question anything or anyone that says that Orlando is more southern than Opelika.

To avoid combing through old yellow pages by hand, we opted to use today's technology, and downloaded all of these businesses directly from ReferenceUSA, a database of business and residential information. Due to its comprehensiveness and reliability, ReferenceUSA is increasingly used in studies that measure the frequency of business names to identify regional identification (Mann 2010; McEwen 2014). Once we had identified the names of the businesses, we then collected other pertinent information on each of the 20,505 "Dixie" and "Southern" businesses using ReferenceUSA. By gathering this business-specific information (the age of the business, the size of the business, the industry sector of the business, etc.) we investigated the degree to which "Dixie" and "Southern" businesses share similarities and differences. This, in turn, gave us a deeper and more complete understanding of southern identity today.

Finally, we contacted a group of "Dixie" and "Southern" business owners and asked them about, among other things, what their business name represents, why they chose it, whether they had considered changing it, and a number of other questions about both the business and themselves. We include these interviews here to help us better understand business naming, as well as the differences between "Southern" and "Dixie" businesses.

Where Is the South Today?

Map 2.1 displays the prevalence and geographic distribution of D scores, and map 2.2 shows the S scores, using our newly collected data. We fill in the areas between cities using a statistical technique that allows us to make educated guesses about the places in between cities to produce estimates of what the D and S scores look like in these places.[3] Whereas most previous work used cut points that remained constant over time to differentiate the

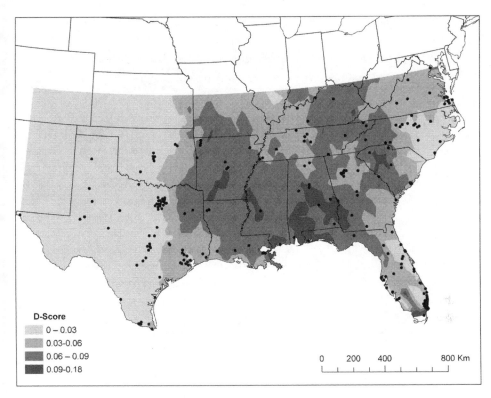

D-Score
0 – 0.03
0.03-0.06
0.06 – 0.09
0.09-0.18

0   200   400   800 Km

MAP 2.1 D score map

shading on the map, we deviate slightly from that practice and instead simply divide the D and S scores into four equally spaced quartiles; higher intensity is represented with darker shading.

The pattern that we see in map 2.1 reinforces the "islands of Dixie" identified by Ambinakudige (2009). Although the largest concentration of "Dixie" businesses is present in the Deep South states of Mississippi, Georgia, and, particularly, Alabama, there are small islands that pop up in western Arkansas and Louisiana, into southwestern South Carolina, and in small pockets in Tennessee. It is important to keep in mind that although there are certainly places of dark shading on the map, even the top quartile represents an extraordinarily small frequency of "Dixie" businesses. In fact, the upper quartile spans from just .06 to .14—representing a range of 6 "Dixie" businesses for every 100 American businesses at the low end to 14 "Dixie" businesses for every 100 American businesses at the high end. Again, this is much different than Reed's (1976) original D score map where all of Alabama and Mississippi, and most of Georgia, South Carolina, and Tennessee

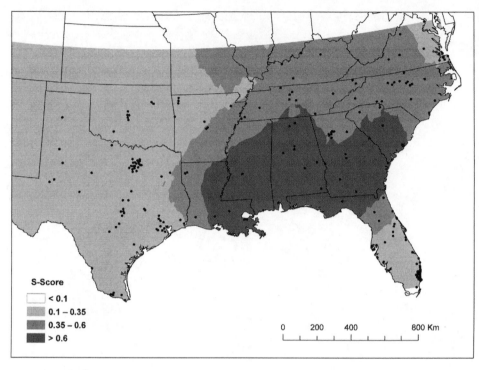

MAP 2.2 S score map

were in the highest category. The state of Mississippi had among the high-
est D scores, with a range of interesting business names, including the
Dixie Baptist Church in Hattiesburg, Dixie Spirits in Biloxi, Dixie Devil
Tattoo in Ocean Springs, and Dixie Bail Bonding, with locations in both
Iuka and Pascagoula. Despite the fact that some of these islands of Dixie
exist, Dixie businesses continue to be fairly rare.

Map 2.2 demonstrates a much more uniform distribution of "Southern"
businesses. There are no "pockets of Southern," but instead wide swaths of
geography that have higher S scores and, presumably, more New South
representation. Not surprisingly, the strongest representation of S scores is
found in the southern portions of Alabama and Mississippi, with some
spread into the Florida panhandle, and small bits of Georgia and Louisiana.
The next highest quartile sits just to the north and encompasses the rest of
Alabama, and much of Mississippi, Georgia, and South Carolina. The third
quartile includes most of the remaining traditional definition of the South,
and the smallest quartile can be found in Texas, South Florida, Oklahoma,
and Arkansas. The same caveats that we used for the D score map are not

necessary for the S score map. In fact, the upper quartile (with the darkest shading) represents places with a ratio of 90 "Southern" entries for every 100 "American" entries on the low end and a whopping 138 "Southern" entries for every 100 "American" entries on the high end. Our findings here were similar to Reed's 1976 work.

Moving away from our maps and considering these scores in totality, we find that "Southern" businesses are represented in much greater numbers than "Dixie" businesses. In fact, we find seven times as many "Southern" businesses as "Dixie" businesses. That translates to an average D score of .045 and an average S score of .40 per city.

Comparing these D scores to data from the past indicates a precipitous decline in D scores, while S scores have remained relatively constant. There were 17 "Dixie" businesses for every 100 "America" businesses in 1976, 9 in 1988, 7 in 2008, and about 5 per 100 today. S scores, on the other hand, have not experienced any decline—moving from about 38 per 100 in 1976 to 36 in 1988, 35 in 2008, and 45 for every 100 today.[4] In sum, "Dixie" has never been as prevalent a name as "Southern," and that distinction has only grown over time. The "Southern" name, however, has remained a popular choice among business owners.

While we have analyzed the prevalence of D and S scores, we have not yet provided a sense of whether they are closely related. In other words, we do not know if D and S scores rise and fall in tandem, or if when one rises, the other one falls. When we conduct this analysis, what we find is a clearly declining connection over time. This suggests that D and S scores have much less to do with one another than they once did. It is less likely now that a city with a high D score will also have a high S score than it was a few decades ago. The substantive importance of this finding is clear: the Old South and the New South, while not completely distinct, are growing farther apart. Moreover, this is one of our first clues about how southern identity has changed and suggests, in part, that there are different ways to think about the South.

These maps and figures give us a good sense of overall patterns, but without other techniques, it is difficult to discern whether there are other factors that may help explain which places are more (or less) likely to have "Dixie" and/or "Southern" businesses. Therefore, we estimated a series of statistical models to determine whether a city's education level, racial characteristics, and population density are related to a city's D and S scores. For readers who want more detail about our model estimations, please consult the appendix.

In general, we find that both D and S scores are most prevalent in areas with the largest African American populations. This is consistent with many of Key's (1949) findings about the importance of black-white relations to southern politics and society. Of course, the areas with the largest black populations also tend to be located in the Deep South and are places where we'd expect to see the largest presence of southern identity, regardless of race. We find that these areas with the highest black populations may see more "Dixie" businesses, but the number of "Southern" businesses is exponentially greater. On average, the difference between the S score and the D score would be .07 larger in a city with a black population of 30 percent than in a city with a black population of 20 percent. It is difficult to know why we see this difference, but we suspect it is because of the negative and often racially tinged stereotype associated with the word "Dixie." Perhaps as a result, several of the "Dixie" business owners we spoke with shared that they had considered changing their name. As one "Dixie" business owner told us, "The business was started in the 1940s by a white southerner [and] was geared to bury blacks. In 1946 my grandfather and a partner purchased the business and elected not to change the name. I followed suit due to the history. Our clients have not shown a negative impression but I have heard from blacks outside of the community who say negative things about the name. . . . If I expand the business I will consider changing the name."

We also find that, all else being equal, S scores are higher in places with a more educated population, but education does not have any influence on the prevalence of D scores in a city. Education is also positively correlated with the difference between S and D scores. In addition, we discovered that there are lower D and S scores in cities with higher population densities. Lastly, population density is lower in places with a greater difference between S and D scores.

In all, this investigation suggests that there is some method to the madness in the ways that "Dixie" and "Southern" businesses are distributed throughout the South. While some characteristics are associated with higher levels of both kinds of identity, education appears to work differently for each type of southern identity. This is an important trend, and one will we return to in the following chapters. While many may associate higher levels of southern identity with undereducated cities and towns, cities with higher education are actually more likely to hold "New South" identification, represented by S scores, and are no more likely to identify with the "Old South," as indicated by D scores.

"Dixie" and "Southern":
Different Representations in the South

To recap, the proportion of "Southern" businesses has stayed remarkably consistent while the number of "Dixie" businesses has declined rather precipitously. The importance of this story rests on the assumption that business owners are expressing their identity in different ways when they choose to include the word "Southern" in the name rather than the word "Dixie." While this makes sense, we have no direct evidence about whether "Dixie" and "Southern" businesses are actually all that different. To discover whether this assumption is warranted, we once again relied on the considerable resources of ReferenceUSA to explore ways the two might differ.

To begin this analysis, we examined the average age of businesses, expecting that "Dixie" businesses would be older than their "Southern" and presumably "New South" counterparts. We discovered that "Dixie" businesses were founded, on average, five years before "Southern" businesses (1969 versus 1974).[5] We also identified several other differences between "Dixie" and "Southern" businesses. For example, "Dixie" businesses were more likely to have a single location than "Southern" businesses, with 93 percent of "Dixie" businesses having a single location compared to 88 percent of "Southern" businesses. "Dixie" businesses were also significantly more likely than "Southern" businesses to be owned by a single individual. We found that 97 percent of "Dixie" businesses were owned by an individual (as opposed to being owned by a firm) compared to 91 percent of "Southern" businesses. Interestingly, there were two Fortune 500 companies represented in the list of "Southern" businesses (Southern Company ranked 171 and Norfolk Southern ranked 247) and none in the list of "Dixie" businesses.

We also find that "Dixie" businesses are less likely to have excellent credit ratings than their "Southern" counterparts (15 percent of "Dixie" businesses have an A+ or A credit rating versus 19 percent of "Southern" businesses) and are less likely to own their property (31 percent versus 63 percent). "Dixie" businesses also appear to have less technological infrastructure—55 percent of "Dixie" businesses have just 0–1 computers, compared to 41 percent of "Southern" businesses. We also discovered some fairly large differences in the percentage of "Dixie" and "Southern" businesses that were closed on Sunday. Only 59 percent of "Dixie" businesses were closed on Sunday, compared to 86 percent of "Southern" businesses.

We suspect the higher prevalence of "Dixie" businesses in retail explains this difference.

If "Dixie" and "Southern" businesses are different, we would expect that they would differ not only in ages, credit ratings, and other indicators, but would represent different sectors of the economy as well. An analysis of business types suggests that this is, in fact, the case. Whereas retail trade makes up 22 percent of "Dixie" businesses, it makes up only 13 percent of "Southern" businesses. Alternatively, health care and social assistance businesses make up the plurality of "Southern" businesses (15 percent); they represent just 5 percent of "Dixie" businesses. We find similar patterns among financial and insurance businesses, which are represented in twice the proportion among "Southern" businesses than they are in "Dixie" businesses. Our data show that there are plenty of opportunities to eat at a "Dixie" restaurant, but it is rarer to receive "Dixie" health care or put your money in a "Dixie" financial institution.

There are, of course, some areas where "Dixie" and "Southern" businesses are similar. For example, we found that 28 percent of "Dixie" businesses are owned by females compared to 27 percent of "Southern" businesses. Likewise, there are no meaningful differences in the percentage of "Dixie" and "Southern" businesses that are home-based enterprises.

Speaking to business owners reveals many similar patterns. Some "Southern" business owners discussed an attachment to the region as their reason for choosing their name (e.g., "southern charm means kindness, goodness, manners, and family roots"), but most of the folks we spoke with gave answers that revolved more around location than identity (e.g., "my business inclusion of the word 'southern' was to indicate where we were physically located" and "southern denotes the region of the country I conduct business in"). Compare these answers to some of the answers given by "Dixie" business owners: "It is a cultural identity. It's our heritage and most northerners wish they were Southern." Another responded, "the words 'Heart of Dixie' used to be on every car tag in the great state of Alabama. That is the reason we chose the name." Yet another "Dixie" business owner said that his name "means my livelihood" and noted that "you might think it's a racial thing but I don't think of it as that." Striking a similar tone, a different "Dixie" business owner said he chose the name "because I'm a southern boy with southern pride." Clearly "Southern" and "Dixie" business owners were evoking different conceptions of the South when they chose their names.

Conclusion

In this chapter, we began to address one of our primary research questions about the resilience of southern identity in light of the political and social changes that have occurred in the region. Based on our findings here, we can say with confidence that southern identity is quite resilient. In fact, our evidence demonstrates that the propensity to identify with the South, as indicated by using the word "Southern" in a business name, has remained constant over the past thirty years. This, by itself, is a noteworthy finding. The South has witnessed massive change during this time period, and despite these changes, businesses still find use in creating and keeping business names that call the region to mind.

Just as importantly, however, we also show that the nature of southern identity is changing. By investigating business names with the word "Dixie," which has always been considered a "meaner word" (Reed 1982, 71) than "Southern," we show that this measure of southern identity is slowly disappearing from the southern landscape. When "Dixie" remains, as in the case of Dixie State University, it is now the object of considerable debate over its meaning.

In chapter 3 we move away from examining business names and toward a different form of evidence, individual-level survey data. This strategy has a number of advantages and also helps us address all of our primary research questions. First, it gives us a chance to add to what we have learned about the resilience of southern identify through our examination of business names. Second, by focusing on the individual level, we have the opportunity to investigate our second and third research questions in earnest: What types of people are most likely to identify as southerners? Why do people of diverse backgrounds choose to identity with the region?

CHAPTER THREE

Southern Identity by the Numbers

T. J. Applebee's Edibles and Elixirs opened just outside of Atlanta, Georgia in 1980, featuring the promise of "nostalgia on a six-laned thoroughfare" (Gordon 1981, 8A). According to one of the two founders, the goal was "to have people feel this is 'their' place, not ours." What began as a single-location southern business soon became a 1,900-restaurant behemoth, stretching the Applebee's name across forty-nine of the fifty states, a few territories, and even some foreign countries. Today, the ironically nicknamed "neighborhood bar and grill" has become a symbol not of distinctiveness, but rather of homogenization.

While Applebee's was marching across the country, other signs of outward-facing regional distinctiveness began to disappear as well. Demographic shifts from rural areas and small towns to urban areas and suburbs also suggested that we were moving inexorably toward a country where vernacular regions were of little importance. In many ways, the suburbs were the ultimate symbol of "Anywhere, U.S.A.," as it became increasingly difficult to tell the difference between suburban Atlanta, suburban Chicago, or suburban Phoenix. The lack of perceived distinctiveness was also fueled by the increasing number of people migrating to the South from outside of the region. This trend is perhaps best illustrated by Cary, North Carolina, where over 70 percent of the city's residents hail from out of state (Governing 2016). Because of this migration pattern, the city has become known derisively by many locals as the Containment Area for Relocated Yankees.

AMIDST THESE CHANGES, we might expect a concomitant decline in regional identity, but our investigation of business names in the previous chapter provided evidence that southern identity remains alive and well. This stability of southern identity does not imply that identity is unchanging, however. Indeed, the current form of southern identity appears to be different than older forms, as the new "Southern" slowly replaces the old "Dixie."

Thus far, however, our conclusions are supported by evidence about business names. While business names provide important clues about southern identity, it is also necessary to consider other types of indicators. Returning to a point we made in chapter 2, business names don't lie, they don't deceive, and they don't give us answers that are socially desirable. But they also don't necessarily reflect the attitudes and opinions of the millions of southerners who don't own businesses. As a result, we shift our focus in this chapter to "regular people" and rely on their answers to survey questions about their conceptions of southern identity. In social-science-speak, we are shifting our unit of analysis from businesses to individuals.

While most readers might guess that this sort of work has been done ad nauseam, the existing survey data on southern identity is a bit scarcer than you might expect. For the better part of the twentieth century, few surveys asked questions about southern identity or the South more generally. The rare national polls that did ask such questions did not include enough geographic southerners to speak with any confidence about opinions in the region. Even when the national polls were large enough to say something about people living in the South, it was very difficult to examine the opinions of important subgroups in the region, such as women or African Americans. State polls had the opposite problem: they provided insights about public opinion in particular states but were not appropriate to generalize to the entire region. In addition to these methodological challenges, both national and state polls were unlikely to ask questions to geographic southerners specifically about the South, and instead concentrated on issues of interest to the entire country, or just one state. In short, for those interested in learning more about southern identity, surveys were of very little help for a very long time. As a result, the study of southern identity was mostly the purview of historians, rhetoricians, geographers, and others who relied on other types of evidence.

Fortunately, beginning in 1991, a few key initiatives began to pave the way for gathering survey data that are helpful for understanding southern identity. Most importantly for our purposes, University of North Carolina (UNC) sociologist John Shelton Reed teamed up with *Atlanta Journal Constitution* (AJC) reporter Pamma Mitchell to create the Southern Focus Polls (SFPs)—a series of semiannual polls investigating behaviors and attitudes in the eleven states of the Old Confederacy, plus Kentucky and Oklahoma (Southern Focus Poll 2016).

As director of the Institute for Research in Social Science (IRSS) at UNC, Reed and his associate director, Beverly Wiggins, agreed to provide phones, computers, software, and trained undergraduate interviewers. The newspaper, in turn, covered the cost of student wages, long-distance charges, and the random sample. Mitchell sold the AJC management on the idea, and the Southern Focus Poll was born. According to Reed, "they got a high-quality poll at a bargain price, and we worked with them to include questions that could make good feature stories for the paper" (Reed 2011).

The partnership led to a unique battery of questions. As Reed noted, "Bev Wiggins and I usually wound up composing the surveys, combining stuff I was interested in, like the southern identity questions, with stuff that would make good newspaper stories, like your favorite baseball team, plans for the 4th of July weekend, and whether you believe in UFOs." After the AJC reported on the results, Reed and/or Wiggins wrote news releases on some of the remaining questions.[1] "A lot of small-town weeklies picked up the stories, and often the AP did too. If the AP took up a story it would pop up all over the country, which provided good publicity for UNC, the IRSS, and the AJC" (Reed 2011).

All good things must come to an end, and the Southern Focus Poll is no exception. A change in management at the AJC combined with rising economic pressures facing print media led the paper to end its support for the Southern Focus Poll. The last poll was conducted in 2001, and no other university or polling group has produced consistent annual data on the South and its people.[2]

Fortunately, the price of polling has declined considerably, technology has improved, and more polling data have become publicly available. In fact, a few recent polls even included questions about southern identity, the Civil War, and the South more generally. For example, the well-regarded Pew Center for the People & the Press conducted a national poll to coincide with the 150th anniversary of the Civil War that included several questions relevant to southern identity, and Public Policy Polling (PPP) created some state-specific polls that included questions about southern identity. Though none of these polls included all of the questions we would have liked, taken together they can tell us quite a bit about the prevalence of southern identity today, the components of southern identity, and the characteristics of people who consider themselves southerners. We can also gain a better sense of southern identity by exploring the level of pride people have in the region and what they think about key events like the Civil War and even the Confederacy.

In sum, the responses to these survey questions tell us that southern identity is alive and well in the minds and expressed attitudes of today's southerners, although the nature of that identity is not monolithic. While we find aspects of southern identity that both white and black southerners agree on, this is not to say that "southernness" means the same thing to both races; there remain parts of being a southerner that are the subject of considerable disagreement. To elucidate the nature of southern identity today, we turn first to the most frequently asked survey question regarding southern identity.

The Contours of Southern Identity

By far, the most common question on these surveys is a simple one: "Do you consider yourself a southerner, or not?" As it is usually asked, this question leaves no room for gradation (e.g., you either answer yes, no, or don't know—there is no room for indicating strength of identification). Despite this potential limitation, the consistency with which the question is asked can lead to some important insights.

As far as we can tell, the first time this question was asked was in a 1971 poll of North Carolinians (Griffin, Evanson, and Thompson 2005; Reed 1983). As many readers know, this was a time of marked turmoil in the South. Busing was, of course, a central topic, highlighted by the *Swann v. Charlotte Mecklenburg Board of Education* (1971) decision that paved the way for busing as a tool for desegregation efforts. Likewise, North-South relations were tense during this time; then governor of Georgia Jimmy Carter remarked that the *Swann* decision was "clearly a one-sided decision; the court is still talking about the South, the North is still going free" (Patterson 2001, 157).

Given this turmoil, we would have expected white southerners to band together and express strong identity with the region. When it comes to the opinions of black southerners, however, it is much less clear what we might have expected. On the one hand, a host of policies designed to improve the condition of blacks were passed in the 1960s. These were highlighted by landmark legislation like the Civil Rights Act of 1964 and the Voting Rights Act of 1965. As Cobb (2005b, 64) notes, "The hard-won advances of the 1950s and 1960s freed many African Americans to embrace their southern roots and celebrate their attachments to southern people and places." In addition, there is evidence that, beginning in 1968 and continuing into the 1970s, African Americans had increasingly positive opinions of "southerners" (Black and Reed 1982; Cooper and Knotts 2006). However, there is also a case to be made that given the continued racial tensions and the proximity to the tumultuous 1960s, black southerners would express lower regional identity during this time period.

Interestingly, the 1971 poll found high levels of identification among both groups, although white expressions of identity were higher than their black counterparts. In fact, 82 percent of whites and 73 percent of African Americans living in the Tar Heel State self-identified as southerners. North Carolina has never been considered a Deep South state, a subregion where we would expect even higher levels of regional identity for whites, yet southern identification is remarkably high in this sample. Indeed, there are very few things that 82 percent of white southerners agree on—not gun control, abortion, evolution, housing preferences, or the designated-hitter rule in baseball. It is certainly telling that the choice to identify with a region yielded this level of agreement.

If the white numbers are a bit surprising, certainly the agreement for African Americans is even more extraordinary. Despite facing daily discrimination, and the visceral reaction to busing throughout the South, almost three in four African Americans in North Carolina identified as southerners. This suggests that only a few years after the tumultuous 1960s ended, the majority of African Americans found a reason to identify with the region.

For the next twenty years, there was scant survey evidence about the extent and nature of southern identity, until the SFPs came along.[3] By aggregating responses to the basic southern identity question in the SFPs, it appears that, in the 1990s, 74 percent of respondents identified as southerners. This is another indication of the remarkable resilience of southern identity, even amid massive population growth. The changes between the early 1970s and the early 1990s are too many to name, but one thing that appears to have remained remarkably consistent is the level of regional identity. One aspect of southern identity that we think changed in this time period, however, was the relative identification of blacks and whites. Reversing the trend from the 1971 North Carolina poll, a slightly higher percentage of blacks (78 percent) than whites (75 percent) identified as southerners in the aggregated SFPs (Griffin 2006). While academics may have frequently treated "southerner" as "white southerner," rank-and-file black southerners had no problem considering themselves part of the regional moniker.

The responses ranged from a low of 70 percent in 1998, 1999, and 2000 to a high of 76 percent in 1995. When we estimate a trend line over all of these years, there appears to be a small, almost imperceptible decline in southern identity of less than one percentage point per year (.7 to be exact). This small decline occurred for men and women, all races and ethnicities, all age groups, for those living in both urban and rural areas, those in the lowlands and southern mountains, and those in the Deep and Peripheral South. Although some scholars argue that this decline is meaningful and "not ephemeral" (Griffin and Thompson 2003, 58), we believe that the changes are less consequential, particularly when considered in light of some of the more recent surveys that we discuss in more detail below.

One reason we question the importance of this decline is that the high point in southern identification from the SFP data occurred not in 1992, but in 1995. Further, in 2001, 72 percent of southerners considered themselves southerners—a number that is only one percentage point lower than it was in 1992, two percentage points *higher* than it was in 1999, and well within the margin of error. As a result, we contend that the story represented in SFP results is one of stability, not change, in southern identity. Indeed, it is remarkable that despite all of the changes throughout the decade of the SFPs—in-migration, the continued rise of the mass media, the proliferation of the Internet, and general modernization and massification—southern identity remained more or less stable. In fact, any decline is more likely a result of measurement error and/or the margin of error inherent in sampling than it is a marked change in southern identity experienced by most living in the South.

Since the last the Southern Focus Poll in 2001, there has not been a consistent source of survey data about southern identity. Nonetheless, we can draw clues from a variety of state, regional, and even national polls. Although they may not have the consistency of the SFPs, they often use many of the same questions and can give us different vantage points to understand the puzzle of southern identity.

Public Policy Polling, a well-known polling organization out of Raleigh, North Carolina, has picked up much of the slack in southern identity polling by asking the basic southern identity question in a series of statewide polls. To the best of our knowledge, the first of the PPP statewide surveys was conducted in Virginia in December 2011. Although Virginia was once known as the capital of the Confederacy, the state has shed much of its southern image—particularly in the rapidly growing region of northern Virginia. If we were to see a precipitous drop in any southern state, it would likely be in the Old Dominion State. Despite this expectation of a significant decline in southern identity, a poll of Virginia voters showed that 66 percent of all respondents identified as southerners (Public Policy Polling 2011). Unlike most other times this question has been asked, however, there was not an option for respondents to indicate "don't know" on this survey. Nevertheless, with nearly two-thirds of respondents identifying as a southerner, this percentage is very similar to the numbers from SFPs, and much higher than most observers would have expected for a state with as many in-migrants as Virginia.[4]

PPP also asked the southern identity question on an April 2013 survey of 1,052 Kentucky voters (Public Policy Polling 2013). Kentucky is an interesting case—it was not part of the Confederacy, but many people consider the Bluegrass State to be part of the South. When you think about it, there really isn't anything much more southern than Kentucky Fried Chicken, the Kentucky Derby, and Jim Beam Kentucky Bourbon Whiskey.[5] According to the PPP survey, 72 percent of respondents in Kentucky identified as southerners, 22 percent did not, and 7 percent indicated that they were not sure.[6] This number is, once again, remarkably consistent with the region-wide numbers reported by the SFPs.

By comparison, a June 2012 survey of likely voters in the border state of Missouri indicated that about one-quarter (23 percent) of respondents said they were southerners, two-thirds (67 percent) said they did not consider themselves to be southerners, and 10 percent indicated that they were not sure (Public Policy Polling 2012).[7] The fact that Missouri, a state that is not part of most people's vernacular region of the South, includes few southern identifiers reassures us that respondents are able to differentiate answers to this question.

These state data, while useful, do not examine the entirety of the southern region. In an attempt to replicate, as closely as possible, the SFP data, we designed a 2011 survey of the thirteen-state South (the eleven states of the Old Confederacy plus Kentucky and Oklahoma) that we called the "Southern Identity Poll," and asked several southern identity questions from the SFPs.

We were particularly curious to see how individuals responded to the basic southern identity question that we have referred to throughout this section: "Do you consider yourself a southerner?" Based on responses from over 1,500 people, 75 percent of people living in the South consider themselves southerners. This is consistent with findings from the aggregated SFPs a decade earlier, and provides additional evidence of the resilience of southern identity. While we are well aware of the potential foibles of comparing polls across time, the consistency across polls and across time is nonetheless striking. It appears that there is a latent level of "southernness" that has existed at roughly the same level since at least the early 1970s. Southern identity is alive and well among people living in the South—in both their expressed opinions and in the names they choose for their businesses. Clearly regional identity is a useful heuristic for many southerners, or else it would have gone the way of Betamax videocassettes and rotary-dial telephones. Despite the resilience of southern identity, this is not to say that the way people relate to the region is not changing. In fact, as we detailed in chapter 2 and expand on below, today's southern identity looks different than it did a few decades before. In addition, we know from the survey results reviewed above that southern identity varies across and within the thirteen-state South.

The Geography of Southern Identity

Although our survey was not designed to tell us about specific states, we thought it would be instructive, interesting, and even a bit fun to rank states by the percentage of folks in the state who consider themselves southern. In addition to giving us a better sense of the geography of southern identity, this demonstration also allows us to test the "face validity" of the data we collected. If we found, for example, that a higher proportion of respondents in Florida than Mississippi considered themselves southern, we might need to go back to the drawing board.

Fortunately, what we found (presented in the left-hand column of data in table 3.1) follows both commonsense intuitions as well as our previous work on place names. Mississippi has the highest percentage of southern identifiers, with 94 percent, followed by Tennessee with 93 percent, and Alabama with 91 percent. The state with the lowest percentage of southern identifiers is Oklahoma, with 52 percent. Other states with lower percentages of southern identifiers are Florida with 59 percent, Virginia with 63 percent, Kentucky with 69 percent, and Texas with 74 percent.

These survey results also correspond pretty well to our previous state-level work on business names. In previous work, we split all states into four categories of "southernness," depending on the frequency with which their businesses included the names "Dixie" or "Southern." With our tongues firmly planted in our cheeks, we then categorized these states as "Southern

TABLE 3.1 Southern identity by state

	Percent Southern	Four-part categorization	Deep South/ Peripheral South
Mississippi	94	Southern to the Core	Deep South
Tennessee	93	Pretty Darn Southern	Peripheral South
Alabama	91	Southern to the Core	Deep South
South Carolina	90	Pretty Darn Southern	Deep South
Arkansas	90	Pretty Darn Southern	Peripheral South
Louisiana	89	Southern to the Core	Deep South
Georgia	85	Pretty Darn Southern	Deep South
North Carolina	78	Pretty Darn Southern	Peripheral South
Texas	74	Not Southern	Peripheral South
Kentucky	69	Pretty Darn Southern	Peripheral South
Virginia	63	Sorta Southern	Peripheral South
Florida	59	Sorta Southern	Peripheral South
Oklahoma	53	Sorta Southern	Peripheral South

Note: The Percent Southern column data come from the Southern Identity Poll conducted by Public Policy Polling of 1,544 individuals in 2011. The four-part categorization is from Cooper and Knotts (2010b), and the Deep South and Peripheral South categorizations are common.

to the Core," "Pretty Darn Southern," "Sorta Southern," or "Not Southern." We classified Alabama, Louisiana, and Mississippi as "Southern to the Core"; Arkansas, Georgia, Kentucky, North Carolina, South Carolina, and Tennessee as "Pretty Darn Southern"; Florida, Oklahoma, Virginia, and West Virginia as "Sorta Southern"; and Texas as "Not Southern" (Cooper and Knotts 2010b). As you can see in table 3.1, these rankings are remarkably close to the ranking of the percent of people who consider themselves southern, although Tennessee does rank a bit higher in our survey than in our naming work, and Louisiana a bit lower. In all, however, the similarities here are striking and suggest that these disparate ways of understanding geographic variation in southern identity produce similar results.

As you look at the ranking of states, you may also notice that the Deep South states (Alabama, Georgia, Louisiana, Mississippi, and South Carolina) tend to have a higher percentage of southern identifiers, while the Peripheral South states (Arkansas, Florida, Kentucky, North Carolina, Oklahoma, Tennessee, Texas, and Virginia) have a lower percentage of identifiers. The exceptions are the Deep South state of Georgia, ranked near the middle, and the Peripheral South state of Tennessee, in the second position. These categorizations are reflected in the right-hand column of table 3.1.

In all, this brief exploration of the geography of southern identity confirms, rather than challenges, many of our preconceived notions about the South. Floridians are indeed less likely to identify as southerners than residents of most of its neighbors (who lie, ironically, to the north). Mississippi and Alabama are also, not surprisingly, represented at the high end of the southern identity scale—regardless of the measure. At the same time, this table displays the considerable differences among southern states. Southern identity is not constant across place and space. While we talk in this book and elsewhere about "the South," anyone interested in the region, its politics, and its culture should be aware that there are multiple Souths. Just because southern identity is resilient does not mean it holds at the same rate across the wide swath of land known as the geographic South.

The Outlines of Who's a Southerner

Thus far, we know that southern identity—at least using this basic question—is fairly stable across time, but still varies considerably across space. One advantage of survey data, like the kind we report here, is that we can also discover patterns in the types of people who are more likely to hold various opinions. As you might expect, most surveys asked a range of questions, so we are able to take the responses to other questions, particularly demographic questions, to get a better understanding of the types of people who are (and are not) likely to identify with the region and therefore address the book's second research question.

We also compare the results from our 2011 Southern Identity Poll with our analysis of the 1992 SFP. Given all of the changes in the region and the country more generally, it makes sense that some of these factors might have changed in importance over time. For example, as the region has moved from two-party competition to one-party (Republican) domination, perhaps the political element has become more important.

In this section, we report results of a series of statistical models that include many potential factors that might influence southern identity, thus allowing us to parse out in more detail whether one concept remains important in the face of all of the others. A summary of our statistical findings can be found in table 3.2. For more details on our variables, coding, and modeling procedures please see the appendix.

TABLE 3.2 Comparing the predictors of southern identity in 1992 and 2011

Who's a Southerner in 1992?	Who's a Southerner in 2011?
Whites	Ideological conservatives
Deep South residents	Deep South residents
Less educated	Less educated
Protestants	Protestants
Long-term residents of the region	Long-term residents of the region

Note: Summary of findings from regression models that appear in the appendix. Data were obtained from the 1992 Southern Focus Poll and our 2011 Southern Identity Poll.

Race

Key (1949) famously wrote that "the politics of the South revolves around the position of the Negro," and, although the language has changed, the sentiment remains. Once we move beyond this basic assertion, however, the story gets more complicated and the scholarly camps less united. Some argue that, given the familial roots many blacks have in the South and the ugly history of racism throughout the United States (and not just in the South), blacks hold no more antipathy toward the South than they do to any other region. Others argue that the South's open and virulent defense of slavery, Jim Crow laws, and de facto (as well as de jure) segregation created a unique sense of antipathy toward the region. It is not much of a stretch to speculate that these two camps might also be divided on to what degree blacks might identify as southerners. Our findings do not settle this disagreement, but provide a bridge between these two opposing views. Specifically, we find that blacks were less likely to identify as southerners in 1992 but no less likely to identify as southerners by 2011. This finding represents a rather remarkable turn of events. While still clearly an important (if not the most important) cleavage in American society, race is no longer an important factor in explaining whether someone chooses to identify as a southerner. The word southerner clearly refers—both in attitude and in action—to both white and black southerners.

Political Ideology

Today, conservatives are more likely than liberals to identify as southerners. However, political ideology was not an important predictor of southern identity in 1992. In other words, in 1992, liberals and conservatives were equally likely to identify as southerners, but that ideological commonality disappeared by 2011. There are a number of potential explanations for this change. It could be that the well-established political polarization that has affected most parts of Americans life has also resulted in an ideological split in southern identity. It could also be that the Republican wave that has taken over the South over the last two decades has politicized regional identity and made it more amenable to conservative Republican residents of the region.[8] Regardless of the reason, it is clear that the relationship between political ideology and southern identity has changed in important ways since the initial SFP, and that this likely plays into the larger regional political divisions that have defined our country in recent years (Black and Black 2007).

Commonalities across Time

People living in the Deep South are more likely to express southern identity in both time periods—even after controlling for other factors. Our finding about the importance of time in region is consistent in 1992 and 2011. Remember that identifying as a southerner is a choice, and this choice implies that people may move from identifiers (assimilated southerners) to nonidentifiers (lapsed southerners), or from nonidentifiers to identifiers. We can't say for certain when this change occurs, but we can say that although in-migrants to the region might not arrive considering themselves "southerners," if they stay in the region long enough, the odds are that they will soon find reason to identify with the region. The prevalence of assimilated southerners might explain part of the reason why, despite significant in-migration to the region, overall southern identification remains fairly constant.

The effects of educational attainment were negative and significant after controlling for other factors in both time periods. Although these results are noteworthy, we do not know whether they are a function of other factors that vary along with education. For example, we know that mobility increases as education increases, therefore, it could be that our findings about education are actually explained by the fact that more-educated people are less likely to be from the South in the first place.

Similarly, the effects of religion are constant across time and across modeling strategies. Protestants are more likely to identify as southerners. Previous investigation of SFPs also shows similar results (Griffin 2006). As a reminder, he aggregated over 15,000 responses between 1992 and 2001 and found that 79 percent of Protestants living in the South identified as southerners.

There were two factors (sex and age) that are not related to the level of southern identity. To many, masculinity is a key component of the South, as seen by the region's stereotypical emphasis on traditionally male-dominated leisure activities (hunting, fishing, mudding, and the like). As a result, some folks might expect a gender gap in southern identity. However, the evidence tells a different story. Even Reed's (1983) survey of North Carolinians in 1971 showed almost identical levels of southern identity between men and women: 39 percent of men displayed a high regional consciousness, and 38 percent of women displayed a high regional consciousness.

As was the case with sex, we did not find any differences in southern identity across our age categories in either 1992 or 2011. Again, there is certainly a reasonable expectation that older people would identify as southern, particularly conservative southern whites who might look back fondly to what they perceive as a bygone era. However, we were not able to find any evidence of a connection between age and southern identity.

Taken together, our findings indicate that: 1) southern identity has remained remarkably stable over time; 2) there is a high level of consistency when comparing the predictors of southern identity in 1992 and 2011 (age and sex don't matter but Deep South residency, Protestantism, length of residency in the South, and educational attainment do influence southern identity); 3) political ideology predicts southern identity now but did not in 1991; and 4) one of the most prominent potential differences (the connection to the region among blacks and whites living in the South) no longer predicts southern identification.

These findings are important for understanding the South, but we are the first to admit that the straightforward question, "Do you consider yourself a southerner?" does not leave much room for nuance. Our investigation can tell us that baseline levels of identification have stayed about the same and that black and white southerners have about the same level of southern identity. Southern identity is a multifaceted concept, however, and to learn more about it, we must consider other aspects of identity and its antecedents.

The Outlines of Regional Pride

One thing that makes studying southern identity so fascinating is also what makes unraveling it so difficult. While southern identity may mean one thing to one person, it may mean something radically different to another. To elucidate what people consider when they think about "southern identity," we turn our attention to various measures of regional pride. Pride is, of course, not a necessary condition for identity, but, as we know from previous work, the two are often associated. As we mentioned in chapter 1, people are more likely to identify with the South when they "perceive it in stereotypically positive ways (and spurn negative stereotypes)" (Reed 1982, quoted in Griffin 2006, 12).

Mirroring previous SFP questions, we asked our 1,500-plus respondents whether "the South has qualities that make it special and different from the rest of the United States." Our results are strikingly similar to those on the basic southern identity question; 72 percent of respondents indicated that the South has qualities that make it special. This is comparable to the 69 percent of SFP respondents from 1992–2001 who believed the South was "special and different" (Griffin 2006). Taken together, the SFP results and our findings cast considerable doubt on the homogenization thesis. In the aggregate, people living in the South still see the region as unique. This perceived uniqueness is a key requirement for the generation and maintenance of southern identity.

Distinctiveness, of course, does not necessarily equate to positive affect. We may very well perceive a culture, region, country, or person to be "unique" but not necessarily mean that in a positive light. To investigate this distinction between uniqueness and affect, we also asked respondents if the South was the best region or whether other parts of the United States were as good or better. Although fewer southerners believe the South is best than who believe the region is unique, we, nonetheless, discovered considerable regional pride, with 60 percent of the respondents indicating that the South was the best region, 36 percent saying other parts of the United States were as good or better, and 4 percent indicating no opinion. Again, to provide some context for this regional pride measure, Griffin (2006) summarized responses to this question based on the three times it was asked on the SFPs. Overall, he found that 55 percent of people living in the South rated the region as the best. Despite many outward facing signs of homogenization, there is little evidence that regional pride—at least using this measure—has declined. If anything, it has increased.

Another way to think about regional pride and the antecedents of identity is to ask how people feel about other southerners. To gain a sense of the way people living in the South do or do not connect to other individuals living in the region, we included another SFP question asking respondents to indicate whether they feel closer to southerners than they do to other people. The question includes a short introduction, "Some people in the South feel they have a lot in common with other southerners, but others we talk to don't feel this way. How about you? Would you say you feel close to southerners in general, or that you don't feel much closer to them than you do to other people?" We discovered that just over half (52 percent) of our respondents said they felt closer to southerners than others. Griffin (2006) also explored this issue and found similar but slightly lower numbers. Specifically, he found that 46 percent of respondents felt closer to southerners than to people in the rest of the country. The stability in this measure provides us with additional evidence in favor of the distinctiveness and resilience argument.

Next, we asked a couple of questions that explore more outward signs of southernness. The first (the southern accent) is not politically controversial but may nonetheless be viewed as divisive. The Confederate flag, on the other hand, is probably the most immediately recognizable and controversial symbol of southern identity.

We discovered that 71 percent of respondents indicated that they "like" the southern accent, 16 percent indicated that they did not like the southern accent, and 8 percent had no opinion. Looking back to the spring 1992 SFP, 82 percent of those surveyed said that they liked the accent, over 10 percentage points higher than in 2011. In fact, this was one of the few questions with a notable decline. People living in the South continue to display southern pride and feel close to other southerners but they appear less fond of the southern accent than they once did. One possible explanation can be found in recent experimental work showing that people with a southern accent are viewed as nicer but less intelligent (Kinzler and DeJesus 2013).

Next, we move to our question about the Confederate flag. While most readers are probably aware of the importance of this notorious symbol, there is much to be learned through a consideration of where the flag fits in the broader understanding of sociology, psychology, and politics. We know that symbols provide simple heuristics that allow people to signal who they are and what they believe in. Given their importance and inherently ambiguous meanings, symbols play an important role in politics (Edelman 1964; Marcus, Neuman, and MacKuen 2000), and we suspect that opinions about the Confederate flag will give us clues about the changing nature of southern identity. Flag controversies flared up in the late 1990s and early 2000s, with particularly heated debates in Georgia, Mississippi, and South Carolina. Confederate flag controversies also emerged following the shooting in

Charleston's Emanuel AME Church in the summer of 2015. Studies explaining opinions about the flag indicate that conservative racial attitudes, conservative political ideology, and lower education levels explain support for the flag (Clark 1997; Cooper and Knotts 2006; Orey 2004; Reingold and Wike 1998). However, we know very little about how support for the flag varies across the entire region, since most studies focus on specific states.

We included a Confederate flag question on our Southern Identity Poll, based on the question that was asked on several SFPs in spring 1993, fall 1993, and fall 1994. The question asks respondents whether the Confederate flag is more a symbol of racial conflict or of southern pride. We also gave respondents the option to indicate whether they had no opinion on this issue. We discovered that 62 percent of respondents said the flag was more about southern pride, 30 percent indicated that the flag was more about racial conflict, and 8 percent expressed no opinion. Even after the Charleston shooting, a CNN/ORC poll indicated that 57 percent of respondents said the flag was more about southern pride than racism (Agiesta 2015).

Comparing our findings to the SFPs results from the early 1990s, we discovered some noteworthy differences in how southerners viewed the flag. In the SFPs, the percent indicating that the flag was about southern pride was relatively constant (70 percent in spring 1993, 70 percent in fall 1993, and 68 percent in fall 1994). Again, in our 2011 survey, the percentage of people saying the flag was more about southern pride was 62 percent, a small decline from earlier studies.

In sum, respondents today are just as likely as respondents two decades ago to view the region as unique, to view the region as inherently "better" than other regions, and to feel close to its people. Opinions about two prominent symbols of southern identity—the southern accent and the Confederate flag—have shifted somewhat. Southern identity is resilient in its broad strokes, but changing in its specifics.

Regional Pride: Digging Deeper

Just as we did with the basic southern identity question, we also explored the predictors of regional pride and opinions about the southern accent and the Confederate flag. Once again, readers can see our statistical models in table A3.2.

Age, gender, and whether the respondent was black do not consistently predict these various measures of regional pride and distinctiveness. We believe the findings related to race are particularly noteworthy. Across four of the five questions, blacks were as likely as nonblack respondents to take pride in the region. The only exception to this pattern is that black respondents were significantly less likely to say that the Confederate flag is a symbol of southern pride (as opposed to a symbol of racial conflict). Given the flag's use by the Ku Klux Klan, as a symbol of resistance during the Jim Crow era, and by a number of other groups opposing civil rights, this is not a particularly surprising result.[9] This is also a key difference between black and white southern identities. While the ways blacks and whites identify with the South are indeed similar in many ways, the differences are important and often lead to political turmoil and continued divisions in southern society.

No matter the question, three factors were consistently positive predictors of regional pride. Conservatives, respondents living in the Deep South, and people living in the South for longer periods of time expressed higher levels of regional pride. In all but one instance, educational attainment was associated with less regional pride, that is, more-educated respondents expressed less regional pride than individuals with less education. On three of the five questions, Protestants were more likely to express pride in the region than non-Protestants.

The Elephant in the Room: The Civil War

In the final piece of our examination of southern identity by the numbers, we turn to our analysis of a 2011 survey from the Pew Center for the People & the Press that coincided with the 150th Anniversary of the Civil War. We focused specifically on five Civil War–related questions: 1) whether the Civil War was still relevant; 2) if the main cause of the Civil War was states' rights or slavery; 3) whether it is okay for public officials to praise Confederate leaders; 4) whether the respondent displays the Confederate flag; 5) and whether someone feels positively when seeing the Confederate flag displayed.

The statistical results appear in table A3.3, located in the appendix. Only three factors predict whether a respondent believes that the Civil War is still relevant. Older individuals are less likely to say that the Civil War is still relevant. It's hard to know for sure what to make of this finding, but one possible explanation is that younger people have more recently studied these topics in school than have older people and therefore consider them to be more relevant. We also discovered that higher educational attainment increased the likelihood someone would indicate that the Civil War was still relevant. In addition, Protestants were more likely to indicate the Civil War was still relevant than were non-Protestants. To our surprise, geographic southerners were no more likely than people living outside the South to say that the Civil War is still relevant.

For the second question, investigating opinions about the primary cause of the Civil War, we identified three important factors. First, it appears that older individuals are less likely to indicate that the primary cause of the Civil War was states' rights. Not surprisingly, race is important here, as blacks are much less likely than nonblacks to say that the primary cause was states' rights. We also found that the more conservative someone is, the more likely she is to indicate the Civil War was about states' rights. Once again, we were surprised to discover that, even after controlling for other factors, the opinions of geographic southerners did not differ substantially from the opinions of respondents who lived outside of the region.

Our next three questions deal specifically with the Confederacy. For the third question, whether it was okay for public officials to praise Confederate leaders, we should note that blacks are much more likely than nonblacks to indicate that this is not okay. Political ideology also has an important effect, as conservatives are more likely to indicate that it is okay for public officials to praise Confederate leaders. Educational attainment has a negative effect on responses to this question, as more-educated respondents are more likely to say that it is not okay for public officials to praise Confederate leaders. Protestants are more likely than non-Protestants to answer that it is okay, and geographic southerners are more likely than people living outside the South to indicate that it is okay for public officials to praise Confederate leaders.

We are also able to identify several important factors that explain whether a respondent displays the Confederate flag. Older people are less likely to display the flag than younger people. In addition, conservatives are more likely than moderates and liberals to display the flag. People with more education are less likely to explain the flag, but after controlling for other factors, females are more likely than males to display the Confederate flag. Obviously, geographic southerners are more likely to display the flag than respondents who do not live in the South.

The final question we investigated was whether respondents have positive feelings when seeing the Confederate flag. Political ideology is one of the most consistent predictors across the five questions, and, once again, conservatives are more likely to express positive feelings when seeing the Confederate flag. Another consistent predictor is educational attainment, and, in this case, we found that people with more years of formal education are less likely to have positive feelings when seeing the flag. Once again, geographic southerners are more likely to indicate positive feelings about the Confederate flag than people living outside the South.

Conclusion

Taken together with the evidence on business names presented in chapter 2, the survey data presented here take us a long way toward addressing the research questions we outlined at the beginning of this book. Our first question asked whether the four individuals profiled at the beginning of the book, Paula Deen, James Clyburn, Natasha Trethewey, and Patterson Hood, were illustrative of overarching trends in the region or whether they were vestiges of a bygone era when southern identity was stronger and more consistent. The results from this chapter show that these folks are the norm, rather than the exception, in the region. Southern identification, therefore, is the rule rather than the exception.

In our second question, we wanted to know what types of people are most likely to identify as southerners and why people of different backgrounds identify with the South. Today, whites and blacks living in the region are equally likely to identify as southerners. This was not true just two decades ago. Although we cannot be certain about the reason for this change, the fact that this change has occurred indicates that the ways blacks relate to the region have likely changed. Keep in mind that identity is a choice. No one is forced to identify with a region. Presumably people only do so if it provides a useful heuristic for understanding their relationship with the social and natural world. It is worth noting that these results mirror what we found in earlier work when we analyzed answers to a question asking people to indicate how "warmly" they felt toward southerners as a group. After years of deep division, whites and blacks in America evaluate "southerners" as a group in roughly equal measures (Cooper and Knotts 2012).

We want to be careful before concluding what this does and does not imply, however. Increasing southern identification does not mean that black southerners are "proud" to be southerners, that they believe the region to be hospitable, or even that they feel closer to white southerners. Indeed, race is still an important and often divisive cleavage in southern life. Despite these differences, however, one thing that black and white southerners agree on is that they are southerners.

Also of note is the changing importance of political ideology. Whereas race is no longer important in predicting southern identity, political ideology has become an important predictor. Just as political polarization has increased ideological differences in a number of arenas, it also appears to have affected southern identity. We suspect that this knowledge may cause liberal politicians on the national stage to appeal to southern identity less often than their conservative counterparts.

Some differences in southern identity have remained constant over time. There remains a significant difference in southern identity between residents of the Deep South and the Peripheral South. In all cases, people living in the Deep South are more likely to express positive identification with the region than are people who reside in the Peripheral South. Social scientists used to talk of inter-regional divisions and often represented this by including an indicator for the South in their statistical models. Although these differences certainly exist, we hope observers of the South will continue to parse out the intraregional differences that are suggested by our findings. Alabama, Louisiana, and Mississippi are much different places than Florida, Texas, and Virginia.

In addition, we discovered that Protestants are more likely to identify as southerners. If the region follows national trends and becomes more secular (Douthat 2007), this finding suggests that identity with the South may decline. Moreover, people with less education identify with the South at greater levels than people with more education. Again, as education levels increase in the region, southern identity has the potential to decline.

Many of the same factors that predict southern identity also play a role in opinions about regional pride, the Confederate flag, and the Civil War. In particular, residents of the Deep South always display higher levels of regional pride than people living in the Peripheral South. Likewise, the time a person has spent in the region is also consistently important when explaining regional pride. Religion and education emerge as important and consistent predictors as well. While Protestants display more regional pride than non-Protestants, more-educated respondents display less regional pride than respondents with less formal education. Political ideology is an important determinant as well, as conservatives display higher levels of pride than moderates and liberals. Race is important in some areas but not in others.

This analysis raises some key issues, particularly regarding race, that we investigate in more detail in chapter 4. Though we find similar levels of identity among blacks and whites, responses to some of our other questions give us some insight into the book's third overarching research question (why do people from diverse backgrounds identify with the South?). It is clear from the results presented in this chapter that, in many ways, blacks and whites think differently about the South. To explore this issue in more detail, we focus on opinions toward important regional symbols that represent identity with the Old and the New South.

Based on our findings in this chapter, we have some preliminary evidence that people are constructing their own definitions of what it means to be a southerner. We also discovered few differences in how members of different races and ideologies identify as southerners, but fairly large differences in how they think about the South—and presumably, their southernness. We believe that identity is more than just calling yourself a southerner. We suspect that different people are connecting to the region in different ways. To learn more about this, we now turn to focus groups.

CHAPTER FOUR

Talking with Southerners

Throughout most of the twentieth century, many southern blacks faced a difficult decision: stay in the South, the region where they were born and where they had family roots, or leave the South to pursue economic opportunities and escape the horrors of Jim Crow. Ultimately, more than 6 million southern blacks chose to leave the South in search of a better life (Frey 2004).

This movement, referred to as the "Great Migration," extended from roughly 1910 to 1970, with only a small dip during the Great Depression (Lemann 1991).[1] The population shift was dominated by low-income blacks leaving the rural South and added a new level of economic prosperity to the industrial, rapidly urbanizing North and West. To be sure, the Great Migration forever altered the economic, political, and demographic makeup of the United States.

To understand the South and southern identity today, however, the Great Migration must be examined in concert with the more recent return migration of African Americans to the South (also known as the "New Great Migration"). Indeed, beginning in 1970, the predominant regional migration trend ceased to be blacks *leaving* the South, and became blacks moving *to* the South (Frey 2004). This trend reached its zenith in the 1990s, when the South's black population increased by more than 3.5 million people (Frey 2001; Hunt, Hunt, and Falk 2008), but has continued into the 2000s (Hunt, Hunt, and Falk 2013).

Participants in the New Great Migration differed from their early to mid-twentieth-century counterparts in several ways. Whereas black outmigrants during the original Great Migration tended to be rural, less educated, and relatively impoverished, blacks who came to the South during the return migration were often economically well off, had extensive schooling, and sought urban or suburban, rather than rural, destinations.[2]

Of course blacks who came to the South were not alone; whites also found good reason to move south during the 1970s, 1980s, 1990s, and 2000s. Their motivations for moving, however, were often different than for their black contemporaries. Whereas whites were motivated primarily by economic interests, African Americans (particularly black females) were more likely to be motivated by familial and cultural rationales (Hunt, Hunt, and Falk 2013).

WITH THIS BACKDROP, we provide evidence from conversations with black and white southerners. This approach provides an opportunity to explore southern identity in greater detail and helps us evaluate similarities and differences in the ways blacks and whites talk about the South and express their connection with the region.

The evidence presented thus far suggests that blacks and whites often think about southern identity and the South in different ways. While these conclusions may be valid, we have not yet presented any direct indication of their veracity and have provided no stories from actual southerners. This is, in many ways, the blessing and the curse of large-scale quantitative data like the kind we explored in chapter 3—they are good at telling us the outlines of the story but not very good at enlightening us about the characters in that story and their potential motivations.

In this chapter, we give voice to a group of self-identified southerners and present their stories, experiences, and views of southern identity and the South. Our objective is to present a more complete understanding of southern identity and a clearer sense of the commonalities and divisions between black and white southerners.

Our Approach

Our task in this chapter is to gather the stories of real southerners and ask them about why they identify with the South and what they consider when they think of southern identity. While it might have been convenient to ask these questions in a one-on-one, completely controlled environment, we were much more interested in exploring them in as real an environment as possible—one with social pressure and social dynamics at work. To understand the importance of this social dynamic, just think about one opinion you hold—this opinion could be about sports, politics, or even the relative quality of what you had for dinner. If you're like most of us, this opinion was influenced by the people around you. You might have considered the information your peers provided, the reactions they gave, and even their body language while forming and expressing your ideas.[3] This is the dynamic we wanted to capture. In short, we wanted to learn about how southerners talked about their experiences with other southerners. This is precisely what focus groups are designed to do.

The idea behind a focus group is disarmingly simple—gather a small number of people in a room, ask some open-ended questions, and watch and listen as they talk about the subject. After the focus group is completed, the researcher transcribes the content and systematically analyzes the results. Of course, while all of this sounds simple, the execution of a good focus group is both time consuming and difficult. Unlike a survey, in which the goal is to represent the population as a whole, most focus groups eschew representativeness in favor of some level of homogeneity, assuming that people will be more open and honest with folks who share their experiences. While we can't realistically prescreen for experiences, we can screen on the basis of demographics—and assume that those demographic differences likely translate to different experiences. And that's what we did.

With all of this in mind, we conducted four focus groups in a medium-sized southern city during the summer of 2014. Although it would have been enlightening to speak with people who lived in the South and did not identify as southerners, we concentrated on self-identified southerners for our focus groups. As we established in chapter 3, this group represents between 70 and 80 percent of people who live in the South, and our primary purposes in the focus groups were to concentrate on *why* this 70 to 80 percent of people choose to identify with the region and *how* these reasons and experiences differ by race.

Because we wanted to learn about how blacks and whites talk about the South, but allow them to do so in the most open and inviting environment possible, we recruited similar numbers of blacks and whites but conducted black and white focus groups separately. This allowed us to talk about potentially sensitive topics like the Civil War, the Confederate flag, and the South's ugly history of race relations without either group having to consider how their experiences were perceived by participants who were members of another race.

Although we have changed the names of the participants to protect their identities, table 4.1 provides basic information on the demographics of each participant, along with their pseudonyms. It may be helpful to reference this table as we progress through the chapter. We have also placed a copy of the focus group protocol and more notes on our focus group process in the appendix. We should note, however, that although we asked each of the

TABLE 4.1 Focus group participants

Participant	Focus group	Race	Gender	Age range
Elizabeth	1	White	Female	18–29
Lynn	1	White	Female	18–29
Brian	1	White	Male	18–29
Mary	1	White	Female	18–29
Stuart	1	White	Male	18–29
Anne	1	White	Female	30–44
Ward	1	White	Male	55–64
Jessie	2	White	Female	18–29
Pam	2	White	Female	18–29
Kathy	2	White	Female	18–29
Emily	2	White	Female	30–44
Alvin	2	White	Male	55–64
Teresa	2	White	Female	55–64
Louise	3	Black	Female	18–29
Peter	3	Black	Male	18–29
Claire	3	Black	Female	30–44
Madeline	3	Black	Female	30–44
Carrie	3	Black	Female	55–64
Keith	3	Black	Male	65+
Cindy	3	Black	Female	65+
Todd	4	Black	Male	18–29
Jack	4	Black	Male	18–29
Justin	4	Black	Male	18–29
Kristin	4	Black	Female	45–54
Heather	4	Black	Female	65+

questions in the protocol, the conversation moved organically into a variety of directions, and not all of these spontaneous topics and probes are represented in our protocols.

After conducting the focus groups, we then identified eight common themes that our participants discussed: "Southern Cultures," "the Conflicted Southerner," "Race Relations," "the Civil War," "the Confederate Flag," "Defending the South," "Changing Identity," and "Looking Forward." These themes guide the discussion that follows. We let our participants speak for themselves whenever possible, and we weave the similarities and differences between white and black participants throughout. Through the process of conducting the focus groups, analyzing the transcripts, and writing up the results, we learned a tremendous amount about how southerners think about their identity with the South—we hope you will too.

Southern Cultures

We began our focus groups with a general question that would allow our participants to become more comfortable with our topic and each other: "What does being southern mean to you?" While scholars have noted that southern identity finds its roots in the South's "fierce commitment to slavery, in its failed experiment with secession and nationhood, in its military defeat and occupation by a conquering power, in its poverty, cultural backwardness, and religiosity, and in its pervasive, prolonged resistance to racial justice" (Griffin 2006, 7), we expected that today's southerners might give us very different answers. We had also expected that we would find clear differences between people of different races and backgrounds. What we found instead was remarkable consistency—across age, gender, and even race. Indeed, virtually every focus group participant described a unique southern culture. As we discussed in the introductory chapter, "if there is a South then the people who live there should recognize their kinship with one another and, by the same token, those who live outside the South ought to recognize that southerners are somehow different from them" (Degler 1997, 7–8). Judging from the perspectives of our focus group participants, there is a South, and self-described southerners believe it is unique. Perhaps most importantly, blacks and whites, young and old, men and women, all cite common touchstones for what it means to be a southerner.

To delve further into our participants' perspectives of southern culture, we organized this section into several categories that were emphasized by our participants: "Hospitality, Manners, and Pace of Life"; "Connection to the Land"; "the Southern Accent"; "Southern Food"; and "Family Connections." We will be the first to admit that this may not look like a particularly important list. After all, these are not particularly divisive issues, nor are they ones that are likely to garner headlines in newspapers, magazines, and Internet sites that report and analyze the news. This serene veneer, however, is misleading. These issues immediately spring to the minds of southerners when asked about what makes them southern. While they may not be newsworthy topics, they are extremely important in helping people construct their identities.

Hospitality, Manners, and Pace of Life

One of the clearest indications of southern culture relates to the "southern way of life." For our participants, this isn't a stereotypical view of an antebellum *Gone with the Wind* South, or one that is defined primarily by combative race relations, but rather one that is marked by hospitality, manners, and a slower pace of life. Many of our participants drew direct comparison to the "North," implying, or sometimes even stating explicitly, that northerners do not hold or appreciate the same values.

As we discussed in chapter 1, there are many reasons to believe that, particularly if they hold negative stereotypes of the region (Griffin 2006), southerners might abandon their southern identity and "lapse." The consequence of southerners writ large abandoning their southern identity would, of course, be consistent with the homogenization thesis. Our participants' experiences and opinions run counter to this view.

For example, Stuart, a younger white southerner who was born and raised in a small town, talked a lot about southern hospitality. He said that many of his perspectives on the region and life were based on how he was raised, "always saying yes ma'am and no ma'am" and emphasizing the importance of courtesy, southern hospitality, and respect for his elders. This sentiment is confirmed by an early Southern Focus Poll, which found that southerners were more likely than nonsoutherners to teach their children to call adults "sir" and "ma'am" (Reed 1993). Brian, another younger white southerner from a small town, also emphasized the importance of "waving at people when you pass someone on the street."

Teresa, an older white southerner, also had an interesting perspective on hospitality and manners. She travels to the West Coast to see her daughter every couple of months and is struck by how manners and hospitality differ between the two regions. She said people are "nice enough, but it is contrived and feels forced. Here, [meaning the South] you are born with it. It is so natural, it is so easy." Emily, a middle-aged southerner, echoed this sentiment, stating "one of the reasons that I am proud of being a southerner is that I don't want to hurt peoples' feelings. I want to be nice to you. When I say 'have a nice day,' I want you to have a nice day. My husband's family [who are from New England]—I can see the satirical, I don't trust you attitude. They tell me not to look people in the eye. Of course, the flip side is that we [southerners] are not sometimes honest with each other because we don't want to hurt their feelings." Ward, an older white male, noted that he "believed that the friendliness in the South was pure, but it was kind of a veneer to not deal with a lot of problems that exist throughout society."

What is striking about many of these comments is how often they define the South in relation to other regions. The South has often been referred to as a "negative reference point" for the nation (Cobb 2005a), but we saw considerable evidence that the non-South, particularly the northeastern states, provided a negative reference point for the self-identified southerners in the focus groups. Clearly, there is a southern "otherness" that persists, even in what may appear from the outside to be an increasingly homogenous world.

We were, once again, struck by the consistency of these comments. Virtually all of our black and white participants mentioned southern hospitality as an important aspect of southern identity, and all used strikingly similar language. Peter, a younger black southerner, said that most people "think southerners (or most southerners) have great hospitality," noting that "they say 'please' and 'thank-you' and 'yes ma'am' and 'no ma'am.'" Another young black southerner, Louise, also talked about "manners and hospitality," and Kristin, a middle-aged black woman, emphasized that being a southerner means a focus on "politeness and manners." This was also the case for Carrie, an older African American, who talked about "manners and the tendency to be more gracious in the South."

Participants in each of our four focus groups also cited the slower pace of life as a key component of southern identity. The importance of this observation was revealed for most of our participants when they traveled or talked to people from other regions. Elizabeth, a younger white southerner, talked about "the slower pace of life that really became clear when I developed friends from New York and other places up North." This experience was the same for Carrie, who said, "When I visit family up North, I notice that my pace is a little slower. We just don't have the same hustle and bustle or urgency, and we can kind of relax. We don't mind if a mosquito bites us." Kristin agreed, noting that "the pace of life is just slower in the South compared to any place else."

It is worth noting that while this may seem like a simplistic or stereotyped view of the South, it is difficult to overstate the importance of hospitality, manners, and pace of life for self-identified southerners. Almost universally, when asked about southern identity, it is these mores and folkways—not politics, religion, or other aspects of southern life—that are at the top southerners' minds. These folkways are not secondary to the experience of southern identity, but rather among the most salient aspects of it.

The Rural South

In response to the aforementioned question about what it means to be southern, many of our participants also talked about a connection to the environment and a rural lifestyle. This is, of course, different from saying that our southerners are environmentalists in a traditional sense. They do not necessarily advocate "green policies," and most are not members of the Sierra Club. Nonetheless, the vast majority of participants cited the land itself as being important to their southern identity. This connection is also frequently tied to the appreciation of rural life that they believe pervades the South. For example, Jack, a young black southerner, told us, "When I hang out with people from the North they are not as rugged. I can walk around barefoot. I guess it is kind of like a country boy type of thing." Justin, also a young black southerner, agreed: "There is a lot of space in the South. There are smaller towns. My mom is from a small town. You have to look quick when you drive by or you will miss it."

Todd, another young black southerner, expressed a similar view, claiming that the politeness in the South has to do with the region's rural nature. "There is a lot of land, and if you haven't seen someone for a few days you are more likely to want to visit with your neighbor."

Stuart also talked a lot about how his rural upbringing affected his identity with the region. He said he grew up in a small rural town with "corn, cotton, one private school and one public school" and noted that "our Wal-Mart opened when I was in high school and my band performed at the opening ceremony." Likewise, Ward, who grew up in rural Georgia, talked about how this experience continues to shape his identity and even the way his children, who are not being raised in the rural South, connect to the region.

While we might have expected these answers from southerners in the 1940s, it is extraordinary that despite rapid urbanization in the South (Lloyd 2012), being "southern" still calls up ideas about a rural landscape. Connection to rural life is apparent to a variety of participants—white and black, male and female, young and old. It is also worth noting that the participants in this focus group were all residents of a medium-sized, somewhat densely populated city, which we might think would predispose them against this rural narrative—it did not.

The Southern Accent

Though our surveys show some evidence of a decline in affinity for the southern accent, we found considerable support for the accent among our focus group participants. In fact, many participants mentioned the southern accent as a meaningful symbol of what it means to be southern. It is important to note that not only did our participants comment on the ubiquity of the accent, they also noted that they *like* the accent. For example, Brian, a younger white southerner, said, "it's easier on the ear, and at work it is easier to disarm people with it because it is not threatening." Most people around the table agreed, particularly as Brian concluded, "conversations just end better with a southern accent." Anne, a middle-aged white southerner who grew up in Texas, told the group a story about how she "used a southern accent in Wisconsin to get out of a speeding ticket." Elizabeth, a younger white southerner with a thick southern accent, concurred and said that in her experience, "people not from here find it charming." One of our participants, Mary, a younger white female, even expressed a degree of self-consciousness because she does not have a southern accent. "People tell me all the time that I am not really southern without a southern accent," she said.

Kathy, a younger white southerner, talked about how people from other regions respond to the accent and suggested that people in the South have to answer questions about their identity more frequently than people from other regions. "Being southern is more of an identity than say if you are midwestern. If you meet someone from the Midwest you are not necessarily going to bombard them with all of these questions. How do you say this, how do you say that?"

Cindy, an elderly African American participant, shared a similar perspective on the southern accent. Like many of the southerners we talked with, Cindy's awareness of and opinions about the accent had their roots in how nonsoutherners responded to it. She said, "I realized that I was a southerner at an early age when I went to visit my cousins in New York. That's when I realized that I had an accent. Other teenagers ask me to say something and they would laugh." Our participants seemed to echo the prevailing wisdom about the accent—that it is the most obvious and outwardly facing sign of being a southerner. Linguist Michael Montgomery (1993, 49) noted, "As long as there is regional consciousness in the South, as long as southerners don't care to be like the rest of the country, and as long as there are efforts to accentuate the regional qualities of the culture, southerners will use a clearly discernible variety of speech that expresses and embodies the regional consciousness and (though it will surely evolve) the southern accent will remain alive and well."

Southern Food

Of no surprise to anyone who follows the burgeoning southern foodways movement, one of the most consistent themes we heard about southern identity related to the importance of southern food. It is particularly noteworthy that we never asked a question about food, yet it came up spontaneously in all four focus groups. The connection between food and family was also important for both white and black participants. This, of course, reinforces many of the themes from the Southern Focus Poll food questions that we reviewed in chapter 1.

For Louise, eating peaches and watermelon from roadside stands is an important part of her connection to the South. Carrie mentioned sweet tea and grits and how food played such an important role in any social event in the South. She also said that "you work so hard Monday through Saturday and you have one day off, you want to celebrate it by coming together with your family. Food was the center of all of this."

Keith, an older black southerner, said that "food matters everywhere but I think there was something unique about the food in the South because it was grown here. Many of our people actually cultivated that food. And they did not have access to certain food and had to make many of these things work. It was about the celebration that brought family together around food. Whenever you went to someone's house, they would always have some food. No matter how poor they were, there was always an extra plate."

Some of our participants shared that food was so deeply ingrained in their family dynamics that certain family members became known for particular dishes. In a defiant tone, Louise said "there is no one who can make greens the way my grandma makes greens and no one can make grits the way my aunt makes grits." Claire, a middle-aged black southerner, agreed. She said that food "gets identified with a particular family member. If you have two plates of cornbread, you know that Aunt so-and-so made this, and Aunt so-and-so made that, and you are going to make sure you get that one before it is gone. It is the way we identify that family time and provides a safe place with no judgment and where everything is surrounded by food."

We heard many of the same perspectives from our white focus group participants—particularly the connection between food and family. Jessie, a younger white southerner, told us about her family's annual beach trip. They rent a big house for the extended family, and her father and his sister plan the menu months in advance. She said that on this trip, "everything revolves around food." There was even some evidence that a rejection of southern food could drive a wedge between family members. Stuart, who had earlier proclaimed, "the more fried the better," felt some sense of alienation from his sister once she eschewed fried food to become a "healthy eater." More to the point, Stuart's aunt is constantly telling his sister, "oh, you like that weird crap." Not all southerners appreciate traditional southern foods, but the ones who do not clearly face a social sanction for their culinary preferences.

Ward also talked about the food tradition in his family. He shared a story about when he was traveling to a cousin's funeral with his children. On the way to the funeral he told his kids, "I can tell you exactly what is going to be on the menu. We are going to have fried chicken, butter beans, peas, mashed potatoes with gravy, and some other meat that we don't know what it is. We are also going to have seven kinds of cake and seven kinds of pie as well as biscuits and corn muffins. And I was right."

For Kathy, food represents a chance to bond with people from outside the region and provides an opportunity for them to learn more about southern culture. "I had a friend here from Oregon who was only in town for one year for a job. He had lived in Southern California and Colorado but this was the first place he ever lived in the South. We would want to go eat out all the time and he always wanted to try new things." She said that her friend once told her, "I just love how much you love food down here."

There were some participants who argued that the emphasis on food, particularly this connection between food and family, may be fading in the South. Ward compared the way he grew up to the way his own children are being raised. He said that "my kids don't have the connection to southern food. Both parents work and this was not the case when I was a kid. A generation back, grandmother made biscuits every day. We are lucky if we fix grits and eggs once a week. The stuff I had growing up—fig preserves, biscuits with butter, scrambled eggs with thick bacon and coffee milk—just isn't part of my kids' lives." Brian concurred, noting that "we always ate family dinners in front of the TV." It is important to note that while some sensed a waning importance of southern food, the majority of those who held this view considered this a lamentable trend.

In all, the experiences of our focus group participants seem to reinforce the themes about southern food that we identified in chapter 1.

Many of our focus group participants expressed a similar sentiment to Alton Brown, who noted that "southern identity doesn't exist without food" (Brown 2014, 32). Further, this connection between food and identity seemed to hold among nearly all of the focus group participants. Although some parts of southern identity drive wedges between white and black southerners, food tends to bring them together. This insight is reflected both in the surveys we reviewed previously and among our focus group participants.

Family Connections

Many of our participants also mentioned the importance of family in creating and reinforcing their identity as southerners. Alvin, an older white southerner, noted that being southern "is about a sense of place and knowing who your people are." Anne expressed a similar view, saying that "people want to know who is your family and what church do you go to."

Emily also spoke about the importance of family, stating that "family is a reason I am proud to be a southerner. I respect my mom and dad. I love my mom and dad. My mom and dad are seventy-nine and eighty-five. I am going to take care of them. Not to say that's a southern thing. But I've seen families in the Northeast that do not do this, some of them. I don't understand it." It is important to note that, once again, the connection to the region is defined largely in contrast to perceptions about people from elsewhere.

This connection between southern identity and family is not just restricted to older southerners, but was also important to the younger southerners we spoke with. Jessie talked fondly about her annual family beach gatherings and said that "we tell the same stories over and over and most of them have to do with being in the South. Family is the main thing for me." Kathy agreed, noting that "people want to know how you are connected."

Whereas all groups mentioned food, references to the connection between family and southern identity were more prevalent in our discussions with white southerners than with the African Americans we spoke with. This isn't to say that family isn't important for black southerners—to the contrary. Family, for our African American participants, seemed to have a closer connection to their racial identity than their regional one. This is just one more example of the complicated interplay between race and region in constructing today's southern identity.

The Conflicted Southerner

Another theme that emerged from our focus groups was the ways southerners, particularly white southerners, were conflicted about the region. Many of the white participants were simultaneously proud and ashamed of being a southerner. Interestingly, the African Americans we spoke with expressed little conflict about their regional identity. They seemed more willing to acknowledge (and criticize) the problems of the region and to separate what they deemed to be the good from the bad. Our white southerners, however, almost seemed to revel in the contradictions that make them southern. As Ward noted, southern identity is about "being obsessed with the past" and the conflicts that arise from "having respect for your family and your past."

Jessie has become more comfortable with her southern identity over the last few years, although she conceded that "the closed-mindedness really bothers me." To illustrate, she recounted a story about a high school teacher whom she called a racist. "He would say that 'not all slaves were unhappy,' find one example from history, and make this a huge focus of the course."

The African Americans in our focus groups did not project the same sense of guilt and internal conflict about being a southerner. They acknowledged and admonished the region's racist history, but they had found ways to simultaneously acknowledge and oppose this past and still identify as a southerner. Once again, this was often defined in contrast to the rest of the country. For example, Keith said that "I never considered myself a southerner until I spent eighteen years in the North. I came back and people called me a northerner. I realized at that point that I was really a southerner." He went on to say that "a southerner is someone who was born here and raised here and caught in that cultural thing in the South. They have experienced all of the region's good and the bad and all of its ups and downs."

Keith also talked extensively about the differences in his mind between being a black southerner and a white southerner. "There is a different view of being a southerner if you are a white southerner than if you are a black southerner. I think many black people were not that prone to say they were southerners based on what white southerners were doing to black southerners at the time."

Many of the younger African Americans we talked with also seemed less conflicted about their southern identity. Todd noted that "you realize that everything you love about yourself comes from somewhere. You don't know anything else." Justin agreed: "Knowing your history is knowing where you came from. If someone attacks the South they are attacking where I came from. Who I am."

For Jack, "every story has two sides. I'm excited that we are warm and happy people but the other side of that coin is dealing with the history that just isn't so awesome for me. Whether I like the South or don't like the South is not black and white for me. There are parts that I like but parts that I don't like."

As we have discussed throughout this book, it is clear that both history and race define southern identity. Certainly this is not news to anyone who studies the South—a region whose past has been famously described as "never dead . . . not even past" (Faulkner 1950, Act 1, sc. 3). What our focus groups uncover that is new and important, however, is how members of different races define and are defined by that conflict between history, race, and the present.

Race Relations

Not surprisingly, race, and race relations dominated many of the conversations we had with southerners. Most of our participants found it difficult to talk about southern identity without at least mentioning issues surrounding race. Our experience with this subject differed from previous scholars (Thompson and Sloan 2012), who reported that race did not come up when talking with whites about their southern identity.[4] Although our participants did mention race, however, many of the whites we spoke with were eager to move past these discussions and instead describe the racial progress over the past few decades in the South. Race was also a powerful issue for the black southerners who participated in our interviews, but they talked about the issue much differently than the whites we spoke with.

Again, most of the whites we spoke with emphasized progress on race relations in the South. Stuart said "things are changing and that it is exciting to see." However, he did note that "it will probably take another twenty years for me not to think white guy or blonde white girl when you say southerner."

Ward agreed, saying that "race is something southerners are obsessed with, either overtly or covertly. When you go into a room you notice the racial breakdown. It is something that we think about. Is it right or wrong? Not really. We actually deal with it better than people in Boston, New Mexico, or Wyoming. The toughest thing is to save the next generation. We are getting more accepting. My children don't have as much of a sense of race as I did growing up."

A few of our white participants talked about racial tensions they faced on the job. Anne, who moved to the area recently, said that she works with a lot of African Americans and that "the racism emanates off of them and that it definitely goes both ways." She said that her job involves "getting African American parents to trust me and it is very difficult. I think a lot of it has to do with the color of my skin."

Lynn, a younger white female, agreed, saying that many "African American women don't trust me." She shared a story from early in her career. "When I started my position I worked with two older African American women. They did not go to college and did not have an education. When I got promoted they were not nice to me at all. I felt like this was racism."

Pam, a younger white southerner, talked about an African American student in her high school English class. He would constantly say, "my people were oppressed, and I would tell him that you are not the only culture, or ethnic background, that has been oppressed. There is the Holocaust. This is the 2000s. You shouldn't be bringing up slavery."

This desire to move past previous racial tensions came up again in a later discussion with Pam. She said, "My grandfather grew up poor in another country. He did not have money for shoes until he was twelve years old, and when he got shoes they were girl's shoes. He would hide them because he was embarrassed. He was very poor but made something of himself in the restaurant business. Everyone comes from different backgrounds so don't use the slavery card to make people feel bad. There are all types of people all over the world who come from bad situations; if you want equality, then stop bringing race up."

Again, there was a much different perspective from the African Americans in our focus groups. Keith, who lived part of his life outside the South, talked extensively about the continuing legacy of race. "Integration has never happened: we've desegregated some institutions, but we have not integrated them." He also noted that "there is as much prejudice in New Jersey and Connecticut as there is in the South," and commented that "the flavor of racism and the flavor of race remains the same, it's a little better but there are still pockets of racism that exist in this country."

Carrie concurred. "I would agree with the fact that racism is alive and well. Kids are segregated by vouchers, private schools, and specialized schools. It's just another form of racism where poor kids get left behind and don't get the education they should get."

Not surprisingly, our African American participants were much more likely than the white participants to talk about race and how they had personally dealt with racial discrimination. Madeline, a middle-aged black southerner, shared two powerful stories about race relations in the modern South. She attended the funeral of her mother's longtime boss. Her mother worked in the school system and was very close to the woman who passed away. A person came up to Madeline and her mother and asked, "Were you her nurse?" Madeline and her mother left abruptly, and she continues to be upset about the encounter. She remarked, "Why did she have to have the assumption that with us being the only black people in the room we had to be the caretaker? Why couldn't I have been her doctor? It's that stereotype. The assumption of what the roles are."

Madeline recounted another story about her work as a real estate agent and a tax preparer. "I did real estate and taxes for years. When looking back, I'd say that 90 percent of my white clients were not from the South. Every real estate transaction I had that was not with a black person was not with someone who was from here."

Peter, an assistant manager at a recreation facility, also talked about situations where race played a key role in his job. "Our clientele is mostly white and when they have problems they don't even talk to me. When they see that both the assistant manager and manger are black, they just walk away. Patrons go straight to the top, and they don't feel like I can do my job because I don't look like them."

Claire also talked about how race was a factor when she was at work. She is a development officer for an educational institution and said, "The good old boy system is alive and well. I am the only African American in my job and we have a mostly white alumni base. When I ask the younger donors to lunch, they will usually go. When I ask the older guys, they won't."

At a later point in the conversation, Keith again reflected on the racial progress in the South. "Even though racism still exists, it is not quite as ugly and as blatant, as malicious as it used to be. The southern people will adhere to the law for the most part. At least they don't go around snatching people out of their homes and killing them and the law doesn't do anything about it. At least black people in the South feel safe again." He then shared a realization that came to him shortly after the 9–11 tragedy. "That was the first time white people in American felt unsafe. Well, black people were terrorized from the beginning of time they were here."

Reflecting more on race relations in the South, Keith said, "Our state has been on the wrong side of history about almost everything. Our state amazes me because white people in our state will do what is not in their best interest because it looks like it has something to do with black people." As an example, he referenced the recent decision to refuse Medicaid expansion in his state, noting that "that is something that will help black people but there are actually more poor people that are white in our state."

Based on our focus groups, there were some signs that race relations might improve in the future. Mary, a younger white southerner, talked about how she and her friends used humor to address the uncomfortable issue of race. She agreed that "sometimes black people do not like white people and white people not like black people. But I work with people in my generation and we joke around about race. 'You are just saying that because I am black.' 'You are just saying that because I am white.' "

Keith talked about the future as well, noting that "young black people and their young white friends will help change the landscape. When I was younger people did not talk about race. Black people were afraid, and white people were ashamed. I think there are going to be some changes in the South, but it is going to take time. There are some people we have to get rid of. Some people have to die. They will be replaced by people who think differently about race and economics."

Ward also ended one of our discussions about race on a morbid note, saying, "Some people are going to have to die for racism to go away." Clearly our respondents struggle with the region's long history of racism. Although some of them think the region writ large can change, they are less optimistic about the potential for individual southerners to change. Instead, they believe that change will come through generational replacement and population shifts.

As we mentioned previously, Key (1949, 5) explained that "politics in the South revolves around the position of the negro." Our focus group participants—who, it is worth noting, were participating in a conversation more than sixty years after Key wrote his treatise—echo much of this sentiment. Although it may be a bit of a stretch to say that the construction of southern identity *revolves* around race, race is certainly tightly intertwined with southern identity for most, if not all, of the participants in our focus groups. It remains difficult, if not impossible, to talk about southern identity without talking about race.

The Civil War

As we discussed in chapter 1, W. J. Cash ([1941] 1991) was one of a number of scholars who believed that southern identity would always be defined at some level by the Civil War. A similar view has been expressed by more contemporary scholars such as David Goldfield (2002), who notes that, at least metaphorically, many southerners are *Still Fighting the Civil War*. With monuments to Civil War battles, schools named after Confederate generals, and a host of other daily reminders of the "Late Unpleasantness" represented on the southern landscape, it is probably not surprising that we felt the need to ask our focus group participants how much the Civil War was part of their southern identity.

No one arrived at our focus groups dressed in Confederate attire, but white participants nonetheless expressed much more positive opinions toward the war and its role in their lives than black participants. Elizabeth recalled history lessons growing up and said, "Our hands-on history had a lot to do with the Civil War. Someone who did reenactment would come to our class." Kathy also held a positive, if not personal, view about the war, saying that "I think there are a lot of southerners who still identify with it, but I don't personally identify with it. I like to learn about it and hear about it, but I do not personally identify with it."

Teresa noted, "I am proud of the war, it's a historical fact. I may not like it, but I am proud of it." Mary was also relatively positive about the war, noting that "the Civil War is not a part of my life, but it is a great story to show people from out of town," and that "it does not affect me personally."

When asked about whether the Civil War is part of their southern identity, black participants provided much different responses. Keith remarked that "the war was just a big mess with a lot of white people killing each other with no idea why they are killing each other. Less than 10 percent of southerners owned slaves." He went on to say that "historians and residents of this state try very hard to pretend that the war was not about slavery, yet, the articles of secession talk about slavery."

Younger black participants also shared information about the ways they think about the war. Jack said that "while the South is known for history, it is not so nice for everyone." Todd was also quite circumspect about the Civil War, the legacy of slavery, and their aftermath. He noted, "We live in the unique situation in the South where we now live side by side with the people who were the oppressor. We don't have that large population of Asians or Hispanics [in the South]. It is mostly black and white. We are face to face."

If food brings white and black southerners together, the same cannot be said of the Civil War. This distinction underscores a major point of this chapter—and this book: the diversity of experiences of black and white southerners means that although there are aspects of southern identity that may draw southerners together, there are, and will likely remain, other aspects of southern identity that drive these groups apart.

The Confederate Flag

Of course, no examination of southern identity would be complete without considering perhaps the most ubiquitous symbol of southern identity—the Confederate battle flag.[5] The flag is the most notable symbol of the Old South and carries a variety of meanings for people currently living in the region. For some, the flag represents southern heritage and celebrates the soldiers who fought for the Confederacy in the Civil War. For others, the flag is a symbol of hate and represents lynching, the Ku Klux Klan, and opposition to civil rights. A third group, of course, may hold opinions that fall in between these two extremes. No matter the position, all of these three groups would likely agree that the flag has been the source of considerable controversy and is often used to represent a particular form of southern identity.[6]

Most of the African Americans we spoke with had an immediate, almost visceral reaction to the Confederate flag. Claire remarked that "it feels like the Civil War is still going on today," and shared a story in which she recently encountered someone with a Confederate flag tattoo. "You want to make eye contact and say hey, you see me. I just decided to go completely around the person just because you don't want to be bothered." Later in the conversation she said that "[white] southerners lost the war but they can still win by wearing the flag," and followed up by noting that "it is more the thing that they don't know what it represents that aggravates me. The fact that they are so adamant to be behind something that stands for something that is negative just because you can."

Louise noted that "I have had so many arguments with white folks about the Confederate flag. They say it represents rebellion. Am I just going to tattoo swastikas all over my body? It is a representation of hate." Carrie agreed: "It seems like it is never ending, trying to preserve something that does not need to be preserved."

Jack expressed a similar opinion. "The flag represents a very old mind-set. I try not to let it bother me. It's an old mind-set that I don't think is very conducive for someone like me to be around or put myself in that position." Todd agreed: "If you make that effort to put that on your car or wear a shirt with a flag, as many places as there are to buy clothes, you are representing something and you want people to see it."

Heather, an older black woman, shared a powerful story about the Confederate flag. "I was driving down the interstate and I saw a Confederate flag on an eighteen-wheeler. I got scared. I had to get away, so I exited the interstate and took an alternative route. When I see that flag, I think somebody is going to hurt me. I don't know where they want us to go. We were born here."

The visceral reaction among black participants was not completely universal, however. Justin said that "I don't really pay attention to the flag. If that is what you believe I feel sorry for you that you even have that mindset, but I believe everybody is created equally." Keith expressed a similar view: "I've dismissed the flag because it does not affect my life at all."

There was much less emotion when whites were asked about the Confederate flag and the role it plays in southern identity—almost as if they were trying to separate the flag from their own identity with the region. Brian said, "I never associated it with slavery because my parents never associated it with slavery. I associate it with nothing." Lynn agreed: "I don't think about the Confederate flag at all. It does not mean much to me."

Other white participants expressed more empathy for blacks when it came to the Confederate flag. Mary does not like the flag, in part "because other people are so passionate about it, it does not need to be there," and continued by saying "I would never have one because it makes other people uncomfortable."

Elizabeth shared a story about her evolving views about the flag. "I grew up thinking heritage, and I remember one time when my brother wanted a flag. My dad said he would get him one, but my mom said absolutely not. She reminded my dad that we have an African American maid that comes to our house twice a week and that this would make her uncomfortable. That was the first time I thought that it is more than a heritage symbol."

Stuart also drew a connection between the flag and racial attitudes. "Racism is still alive and well. Growing up you would see the flag. You would see it on a car or on someone's front porch. You would engage with these people and racial remarks would be made. When I see flag, I think negative."

It is probably not surprising to most readers that the flag remains a divisive symbol and that the black and white southerners in our focus groups hold different views about the importance of the Confederate flag. What was surprising to us, however, was not the valence of opinions on the flag for white and black southerners, but the strength of these opinions. Our white southerners responded to the controversy over the flag not by defending its centrality for their identity, but instead by downplaying its importance. They may have supported their right to fly the flag, but they did not define it as a central component, or even a crucial symbol, of their southern identity. Generally speaking, our black participants had more consistent, negative opinions of the flag, and, with one notable exception, continued to highlight its importance in their lives. If this finding can be generalized to others outside of our focus groups, it may explain why the Confederate flag seems to be fading in the South—at least in government-sponsored venues, such as state capitols, and when represented on state flags.[7] As a wealth of research in political science has taught us, when an issue is salient to one group (as the flag is to blacks) and is less salient to another group (as the flag seems to be for many whites), we would expect the former group to ultimately achieve policy success.

Defending the South

One of the more surprising discoveries from talking with southerners was how much of their southern identity is defined in contrast to people from other regions. Almost everyone we spoke with was frustrated and embarrassed with how southerners were portrayed in the media. In addition, a number of participants shared stories of when they had gotten particularly defensive about the South and their identity as a southerner. In many cases, this defensiveness occurred when interacting with people from outside the region who were critical of the South or southerners.

Louise reflected a common critique of the media among our participants, claiming that "the media can't wait to report on bad things going on in the South." Madeline agreed, focusing specifically on the recent spate of southern-based reality television shows and saying that they "reinforce stereotypes of southerners not being as smart."

Jack concurred. "I defend the South when someone who is not from here makes a comment." He went on to say, "Things on TV makes us appear like we are dense and not as smart or fashionable as people in the northern states. My friends from the North make jokes like it's cool to marry your cousin down there." He also shared a frequent occurrence on social media that raises his ire. "Someone will put a new article on Facebook that is something bad someone in the South did. I'm slapping my head more than I am beating my chest."

Like Jack, Elizabeth also referenced the way the South is portrayed on social media. She said that a constant occurrence on Facebook is for a friend to say, "Hey watch this funny video of a person saying something completely idiotic," and remarked that "nine times out of ten they are from the South."

Justin even spoke out in defense of the clothes southerners wear. "Certain people up North have a perception about how we are down South. We might wear long sleeves with some shorts, and they might say that this is weird. Or you might wear sandals with socks on, and they will think that is weird. Just because we don't do the same things they do, they think it is just wrong."

Keith provided some keen insight on when he is willing to defend the South. "I have never been ashamed to say I was a southerner, because I sep-arate being a black southerner from being a white southerner. The white southern people act crazy. The reason I was always proud of being a black southerner is that when you look at the black women or black men who changed America, most of them were educated in or brought up in the South." Recalling his time as a teacher, Keith noted that "I used to tell my students that if you can name four African American men or women who did anything significant and were not educated in the South or born in the South I will give you an 'A' in the class and you don't have to come to class anymore. I have always been proud to be from the South because I look at the black men and women from the South. Now I am a little embarrassed about the white folks who come from the South."

White focus group participants also reflected on the way the South is portrayed in the media. Kathy talked about Bravo's reality television show *Southern Charm*. "During one of the first episodes, they showed a dinner conversation where the women debated whether they would pick Ashley Wilkes or Rhett Butler from *Gone with the Wind*. I mean, we don't sit around talking about *Gone with the Wind* all the time at our plantations. I promise this is not what the South is like."

Ward lashed out at the media but pointed to a time before the advent of reality television. "One of the worst things that ever happened to the South was the *Dukes of Hazard* T.V. show." He also shared a running joke he has with a friend about the way the South is portrayed in the media. "Every time our state is in the *New York Times* it is a bad story. You can also extend this to Jon Stewart. Every time our state is on *The Daily Show*, it is not some-thing flattering.[8] People do get the predisposition that we are a bunch of idiots. This is reflected in the headlines of these news and joke news sources. It's embarrassing."

Kathy agreed. "When there is a news story, they find the dumbest hick with the fewest teeth they can. This is how the rest of the country ends up perceiving the South. There are plenty of racist people, there are plenty of uneducated people, but there are plenty of those people everywhere. There is a tendency for the media to focus on the negative in the South." Alvin agreed. "Hollywood's renditions make me embarrassed to be a southerner."

For some, defending the South extended past stereotypical media portrayals. This was a particularly important issue for Alvin, a lifelong southerner:

> One of the things I resent is people not from the South coming
> here with preconceived notions about how little change has taken
> place. Even when they are reminded of those changes or when those
> changes are pointed out, they are not willing to give any due credit
> or concessions. I am sick and tired of missionaries, desk missionaries,
> coming here with briefcases from more than 50 miles away. They
> have been to the mountaintop. They are going to tell us how back-
> ward we were. Some of them have more deep-seeded prejudices and
> bigotry than I ever knew of my grandparents.

Alvin had tears in his eyes when he talked about the pride he had during the 2008 presidential primary. "I watched Barack Obama win our state's presidential primary with more Democratic votes turning out for that election than had turned out for any primary election in history. That says that we can not only embrace change but we can fight the preconceived notions others have."

Clearly the South and southern identity can only be understood in the larger context of the country as a whole. In chapter 1, we cited a number of scholars who argued that southern identity requires both outsiders and southerners to view the region and its inhabitants as unique. Our participants reinforce that idea and highlight just how sensitive southerners are to how they are perceived.

Changing Identity

One of the benefits of focus groups is that we are able to ask in-depth questions and to talk with participants about how their thinking on a subject has (or has not) changed over time. We were particularly interested to learn more about whether and how black and white southerners' identification with the region has evolved over the course of their lifetimes.

Reed (1983) gives us useful terminology for this discussion when he describes assimilated southerners—people who are not originally from the South but move to the region and over time begin to think of themselves as southerners. Mary is an excellent example of an assimilated southerner. She grew up in the Midwest and moved to the South as a teenager. She said that she was "originally embarrassed to say I was from the South, but then I learned about the history and began to accept the past and realize it was part of the history. Now, I embrace the South."

There were also a number of southerners who felt more identification with the South after leaving the region. Anne was born in the South but moved around a lot in her twenties and thirties. "I've had a love-hate relationship with the South. I vacillate between shame and pride, and it really depends on where I live. I've seen some horrifically racist things in southern states. It has made me ashamed. I have also had conversations with Yankees about slavery. Of course, I have never owned a slave. I will say that we are not the only ones who can't seem to get over the past."

Emily is from a self-described "mixed-marriage" (she's from the South and her husband is from New York). "If you are in another region, people are going to be saying, 'oh, you are from the South.' I married a guy from New York and his parents have a thick New York accent. My father-in-law was surprised I had shoes. I was defending my accent. I was defending everything when I lived in New York."

Even the younger southerners we spoke with shared stories about how their southern identity had evolved over the course of their relatively short lives. Jessie talked about her transition from being ashamed of the South to being proud of her southern identity. "I graduated with thirty kids in my high school class and grew up in a small town. Everyone I went to high school with was a redneck. They did not know how to speak proper English, they did not care about learning, and they did not want to learn. My classmates were ignorant, and I could not wait to get out. When I left high school I was not proud to be a southerner. I distanced myself from the South. This changed when I came to college. It took a while, but now I am definitely proud to be a southerner."

Pam shared a similar story. "Growing up I used to be so embarrassed to be a southerner. My mom is really southern, and she would talk to everyone in the grocery store. She doesn't know how to whisper. I've changed, and now, I talk to everyone I see."

We heard similar stories from several of the young black southerners we spoke with. Louise told us how she

remembered learning about the Ku Klux Klan and segregation in elementary schools. I used to have nightmares all the time about the

KKK and Hitler. I remember my grandparents telling stories about growing up and how they had friends who were murdered. I always felt that the South was not a place that was familiar to me or friendly to me. At my high school, southerners were white, wore cowboy boots, and went tailgating on the weekends. I never identified with the South until I came to college and then started traveling around the United States. I started dating someone from Syracuse [NY], and when I traveled with him to Syracuse, people would comment on my accent and say that it was funny. They would ask me to say something else. I guess it was seeing people from different parts of the country and missing home that strengthened my southern identity.

Claire also talked about the role college played in shaping her southern identity. "I remember being in college and going home with my white friends. I'd attend a Lutheran Church instead of my AME church. These experiences really opened my eyes to different experiences of being southern."

Having feelings of southern identity increase over time was not a uniform experience, however. Jack said that "when I was growing up I thought the South was ideal. Everyone was so nice. It was only when I left my element that I realized this was such a backward way of living." He then shared a story about working overseas. "I thought people were second-guessing me but realized it was because I was carrying baggage from growing up in the South. The South messed me up by making me think that I was not as credible."

For Madeline, her identity with the South has decreased with the polarized politics and the tendency for her elected leaders to bring embarrassment to the region. "My identity has changed over the last couple of years. I am embarrassed by the politics in my state. It makes me feel backward."

Although the specific experiences varied, nearly all of our participants described how their southern identity waxed and waned in its intensity over the course of their lifetime. As we noted in chapter 1, migrants to the South are two and a half times more likely to assimilate if they feel close to other southerners (Griffin 2006). We certainly discovered support for this finding in our focus groups.

Looking Forward

We ended each of our focus group sessions by asking participants whether they think their southern identity will become more or less important in the future.

Some of the participants predicted that southern identity would become less important in the future. Mary said that "the South is dying out. Everything is becoming mainstream. Who's your family and where you are from will be less important for the next generation." Kathy agreed, saying that "people are more mobile today. My dad built a house right next door to his parents and so did his brother. His sister is the furthest one away, and that's forty-five minutes. His cousins, aunts, and uncles are all close by. They moved away for a while after school, but they always came back. People are more spread out now."

Other participants provided a different perspective. Peter said, "Being a southerner will be more a part of me in the future. When I get older and have a family it will be more important. I will tell my kids the good and the bad of how I grew up. I am not ashamed of who I am. If I let me being a southerner fall by the wayside that is not being true to who I am."

Although we do not doubt Kathy and Mary's personal reflections, when it comes to predicting the future role of southern identity, we side with Peter. Our focus group participants have experienced rapid change and homogenization throughout their lifetimes, yet all of them were adamant about their southern identity and its importance in their lives. If "the South" as a concept were an easy idea to kill off, it would be long dead. Instead, as we have shown throughout this book, southern identity is resilient. It may change form, but if history is any guide, people will continue to search for distinctiveness and originality, even in the face of rapid change.

Conclusions

In chapters 2 and 3, we used analyses of business names and survey data to demonstrate the resilience of southern identity. While the stability of southern identity is an important story, our research design in those chapters limited our ability to address our third research question because our investigation was missing the voices of real southerners talking about how and why they choose to identify with the South. We hope this chapter has provided a space for these voices to be heard.

By talking with southerners, we have come to appreciate how much southern identity is developed in response to perceived difference to people in other regions. As Teresa, an older southerner, noted, "being a southerner means not being a northerner." In this way, southern identity and southern behavior more generally are impossible to understand without considering the broader national context. As long as people describe themselves as New Englanders, Midwesterners, and the like, so too will many describe themselves as southerners.

Second, we have learned that blacks and whites think about the South in both similar and different ways. Tradition—a connection to the land, food, and history—dominates southern identity for both groups. Both black and white focus group participants believe that they are southern, and they are generally proud of being southern. On the other hand, the lingering specter of race haunts this discussion. Clearly uncomfortable with the implications of expressing support for much of the region's past, whites are quick to highlight progress in race relations. We saw no evidence, explicit or implicit, among these white southerners that preserving the racial order was "the cardinal test of a southerner" (Phillips 1928, 31). Our black participants, however, were much less apt to highlight racial progress, but simultaneously quite comfortable expressing a connection to the region. While whites may express support, or at least tolerance, for the lingering importance of the Civil War and the Confederate flag, our black participants clearly discount both as important parts of what it means to be a southerner. In sum, our focus group results reinforce both the resilience and the changing nature of southern identity today. Further, they highlight the nuanced similarities and differences between how blacks and whites identify with the South. Blacks and whites both identify with the South at similar rates, but that does not mean that their views of the South are identical. In many ways, the differences between white and black conceptions of southern identity may suggest that the concept of southern identity may best be treated as a plural, rather than a singular concept. Perhaps what we are witnessing, then, is the resilience of southern identities.

Conclusion

We began this book by profiling four public figures: Paula Deen, James Clyburn, Natasha Trethewey, and Patterson Hood. On the surface, these four folks don't have much in common. They represent different races, ages, levels of education, and likely even political perspectives. Despite these differences, each identifies as a southerner and has chosen to make their southern identity a central part of their professional and personal existence. The reasons they chose that identity likely vary, but the fact that they all opted to be known as a "southerner" is important to understanding how people make sense of their place in the world.

We profiled these individuals to jump-start a larger conversation about southern identity framed around three primary questions. First, how typical are these four individuals? Second, what types of people are most likely to identify as southerners? And third, why do people from such diverse backgrounds, particularly diverse racial backgrounds, identify with the South?

The Resilience of Southern Identity

When addressing our first question, we can say with confidence that Deen, Clyburn, Trethewey, and Hood have a lot of company in proclaiming their southern identity. By reviewing a variety of evidence, we find that southern identity is resilient, and there are even some signs of growing connection to the American South. Whether we examine business names, responses to survey questions, or the stories of southerners themselves, southern identity is alive and well in the twenty-first century. Although we limit ourselves to those three examples in this book, the fact is that there are many other examples in modern life that also reinforce the continued importance of southern identity. Southern food has become more popular across much of the country, aspects of southern culture can be found in music and art, and the growing acceptance of southern political rhetoric all reinforce the notion that southern identity is resilient and promises to remain so for quite some time.

Recall that there is long line of people who have argued that southern identity is fading. Indeed, scholars, media spokespeople, and opinionated folks from across the country have been predicting a decline in southern identity for decades. Their logic was seemingly unassailable: What purpose does regional identity provide in a world of rapid and accurate communication across towns, cities, states, and even countries? Add that to an increasingly mobile population and there would seem to be little room left for regional identity. What we find, however, is that many of these changes make southern identity *more* important in people's minds today. Over thirty years ago, Reed argued that "the economic and demographic changes that have swept across the region have clearly *not* rendered Southern identity useless and irrelevant, nor have they doomed it to early extinction" (1983, 108).

Today, we would even go a step further than Reed. Southern identity is not useless or irrelevant, but central to the ways that millions of people perceive their place in the world and relate to each other. It is not an accident that when we meet someone, one of the first questions we ask them is not about how much money they make, their ethnic background, or their stance on presidential politics. Instead, one of the most frequently asked questions is "Where are you from?" (Walsh 2012, 520). This simple, and seemingly unassuming, question underlies the importance with which Americans of all stripes ascribe to their regional homes. The need for people to attach themselves to place in a time of rapid change may have "increased the need for people to draw boundaries, more crisply define their geographic communities, and perform elements of their identity rooted in physical places, such as speech patterns" (Walsh 2012, 520).

A New Brand of Southern Identity

While we are unwavering in our belief that southern identity is resilient, we are simultaneously convinced that ways people connect with the region today are markedly different than they were in the past. Connection with the Old South is indeed disappearing; anyone who doubts this need look no further than the recent furling of the Confederate flag throughout much of the region. In perhaps the most prominent example of this trend, the flag was taken down from the Confederate memorial located in a prominent place on South Carolina's State House grounds on July 10, 2015, less than a month after the Charleston church shooting. In a symbolic and carefully choreographed ceremony, the flag was lowered by members of the Highway Patrol Honor Guard and handed to the unit's leader, Lieutenant Derrick Gamble. Gamble, who is African American, then handed the flag to the state's director of Public Safety, Leroy Smith, who is also black. The flag was then delivered to the state's Confederate Relic Room and Military Museum. This movement of the flag, from an official prominent position to one contextualized as "history," is reflective of broader changes related to Old South identification throughout the region. As this Old South identification declines, it is being replaced, and in some cases surpassed, by more inclusive indicators of regional identity.

This embrace of a new type of southern identity will continue to have a number of important consequences—politically, culturally, and economically. A southern identity defined around Confederate flags, entrenched gender roles, and racially exclusionary policies and practices is certainly fading. And where it does remain, we can expect a concomitant decline in economic prosperity because extant businesses will suffer and few new businesses will choose to locate to an area defined by the Old South.

While there is an "old" to "new" shift in southern identity, this evolution is occurring alongside similar changes in southern music, southern food, and perhaps even southern politics. We believe these changes are both a cause and a consequence of the ways southern identity has evolved and the types of people who call themselves southerners.

The New Southerner

If southern identity has remained while the nature of that identity has shifted, the obvious question moves from the aggregate down to the individual: Who identifies as a southerner? The answers to this question, just like the answers to the question above, provide some counterintuitive trends—particularly when it comes to the effects of age, gender, and race on southern identity. Once we account for other factors, such as the time a person has lived in the region, younger people are just as likely as older people to identify with the South. Likewise, women are as likely as men to identify as southerners. In fact, there are very few examples where men and women hold significantly different views about the region.

Not surprisingly, we found a strong subregional dynamic in southern identity. Even after accounting for a host of factors, individuals living in the Deep South are considerably more likely to identify as southerners than people living in the Peripheral South. The amount of time an individual has spent in the region is another powerful predictor of southern identity. Even after accounting for several other factors, the longer someone has lived in the South, the more likely he is to identify as a southerner. In addition, we discovered a religious component to southern identity, finding that Protestants are more likely to identify with the South than individuals from other religions.

Of perhaps the most importance, we found that race is no longer a significant predictor of southern identity. It is difficult for us to overstate the significance of this finding. In 1992, blacks were less likely to identify as southerners once we accounted for other possible explanations. By the early 2010s, this difference had disappeared. Simply put, blacks today are just as likely to identify as southerners as are whites. Phillips (1928, 31) declared that race was the "cardinal test of a Southerner and the central theme of southern history." Moreover, he predicted that the South "shall be and remain a white man's country." This is not the case today. African Americans identify with the region at comparable levels and connect with the South for many of the same reasons as whites. Anyone who uses the word "southerners" as a synonym for "white southerners" is not accurately portraying the region's modern reality.

Southern Identity in Black and White

Why do people from such diverse backgrounds, particularly diverse racial backgrounds, identify with the South? Whites and blacks in our focus group emphasized hospitality, manners, and the slower pace of life when discussing their southern identity. The black focus group participants viewed southern history much differently than most whites and, not surprisingly, had more negative feelings about the region's past than did the white participants. For example, blacks were less willing than whites to agree that the region had left its past behind. These findings highlight the need for more initiatives like the William Winter Institute for Racial Reconciliation in Mississippi, which is devoted in part to "creating an equitable future by addressing fully, and together, our shared history" (William Winter Institute 2015). Despite this painful history and a legacy of overt discrimination that continues today, African Americans find ways to identify as southerners. Moreover, like the white participants, the African American participants were quick to defend the South against its detractors.

We also discovered that younger African Americans connected with the region in ways that celebrated the positive aspects of southern identity while at the same time acknowledging the region's negative history and continued legacy of racial strife. In addition, considerable faith is being placed in this younger generation of southerners, particularly from older African Americans, to reach across the racial divide and work together toward the betterment of the region.

We looked closely at the views of younger and middle-aged white southerners as well. These individuals grew up after the modern civil rights movement and never lived in a region with laws enforcing racially separate schools, segregated public accommodations, and the oppression of Jim Crow. This group of southerners also emphasized favorable elements of southern culture, including manners, hospitality, and food. These individuals showed an ability to select the aspects of the region that they perceive as positive and, though familiar with southern history, deemphasize certain parts of the past, talk about a need to move forward, and emphasize the importance of looking toward the future. The younger whites in our focus groups were quick to defend the South when the region was criticized by nonsoutherners, public officials, and/or the media.

In sum, black and white southern identifiers talk about the region in many of the same ways, but some differences do persist. For example, both whites and blacks emphasize the importance of family, manners, hospitality, food, and the southern landscape, but blacks and whites do not see eye to eye on the role of history and race relations in shaping why they identify as southerners. Though we did not see evidence that these differences were causing a decline in southern identity, it was exceedingly clear that black and white southerners viewed these issues much differently.

Our conversations with African American southerners helped us develop a better understanding of how blacks reconcile the region's negative racial history with their self-identities as southerners. We confirmed that one of the primary reasons for the high level of southern identity among blacks is that African Americans feel much more positively about the region, and even the term "southerners," than they once did (Cooper and Knotts 2012). The focus groups also helped us understand how some African Americans think about southern identity, with one participant even noting that there was a difference in his mind between being a white southerner and a black southerner. These African Americans have seized the space, not letting the South remain a "white" place.

The Politics of Southern Identity

If race is shrinking as an important cleavage in southern identity, politics may be taking its place. Recall that political ideology did not help us understand who considered themselves a southerner in the early 1990s, but ideology is now an important predictor of southern identity. Our results indicate that conservatives are more likely to identity as southerners than are moderates and liberals. This is a key finding, and one that runs counter to the broader trends we find. In general, southern identity is becoming more, rather than less, inclusive for geographic southerners—men and women, blacks and whites are all equally likely to consider themselves southerners. Politically, however, it appears that the opposite is occurring.

We suspect that this shift may reflect the broader political realignment that has occurred throughout the last half-century. Whereas political ideology and partisanship were once distinct concepts, today liberals are more likely to be Democrats, and conservatives are more likely to be Republicans than they have been at any time in the past. There is even evidence indicating that Republicans and Democrats discriminate against one another to an even greater degree than whites discriminate against blacks today (Iyengar and Westwood 2015). This change is particularly evident in southern politics. For much of the 1970s and 1980s, biracial coalitions of blacks and whites elected moderate white Democrats to office in the South. A host of factors, including the rise of majority-minority districts, the national Democratic Party's move to the left on issues of race, and the popularity of President Ronald Reagan have resulted in a political environment that is much more racially polarized than it once was (Black and Black 2002). Political scientists have even argued that racial conservatism has become even more strongly correlated with political partisanship than it was in the past (Valentino and Sears 2005). For these and a host of other reasons, a plurality of southern Democrats today are black, and the vast majority of southern Republicans are white.[1]

Toward a Theory of Southern Identity

As we suggested at the beginning of this chapter, we have a good sense of the size, shape, and durability of southern identity today. The question remains, however, whether this information helps us develop a broader theory of southern, and perhaps even regional, identity. A theory, of course, is an explanatory framework for understanding a particular phenomenon. Developing the right theory can help us explain the world in shorthand and can provide us with a set of predictions to help us understand what is likely going to happen in the future. While theory building is an important enterprise, it is not an easy one. Like Cobb (2005, 6), we have found that working to develop a theory of southern identity leaves us somewhat "bleary eyed, brain befogged and not much the wiser for it all." Nevertheless, our findings can inch us a few steps closer to a larger understanding of southern and regional identity.

As we noted in chapter 1, there are three reasons someone might identify as a southerner: "[F]olks will more likely think of themselves as southerners if they have a consciousness of the South as distinctive, perceive it in stereotypically positive ways (and spurn negative stereotypes), and identify with and believe themselves similar to others in the region and dissimilar from regional outsiders" (Griffin 2006, 12). The evidence we present in this book, particularly the focus group results summarized in chapter 4, demonstrates that these dynamics continue to take place today. To a person, our focus group participants agreed that the South was distinctive, and, though they were not universally positive about the region, there was a clear sense that the positives outweighed the negatives. Reed's point about outsiders, drawing on the literature emphasizing the importance of in-groups and out-groups in the formation of social identity, was also quite evident in the focus groups. Whether talking about southern hospitality, manners, the region's pace of life, or a connection to family, southerners often discuss these issues in relation to nonsoutherners, particularly people from the Northeast.

In addition, a modern background and set of life experiences can contribute both positively and negatively toward southern identity (Reed 1983). For sure, these factors decrease a person's traditional value orientation. We know that people with traditional value orientations are more likely to identify as southerners. So, how can southern identity be alive and well in an increasingly modern region? We found considerable evidence that these same modernizing experiences also induce an increased regional consciousness (and regional consciousness leads to an increase in southern identification). When people go away to college, travel to other parts of the country (or the world), and interact with people from different cultures, they gain an enhanced regional consciousness, which can ultimately strengthen southern identity.

Our time talking with southerners was particularly useful in helping us better understand how this dynamic can work. Both white *and* black focus group participants talked emphatically about how education and/or leaving the South enhanced their sense of regional consciousness and their southern identity. Some even recalled that they were not proud to be a southerner in high school, but recounted how this shame shifted to pride when they left home, moved away to college, or were relocated to another part of the country. It is this encounter with others that leads people to see that the South and southerners are indeed distinct. It is this perception of distinctiveness that often strengthens identification.

The Future of Southern Identity

Nearly all demographic projections indicate that the South will continue to experience substantial population growth and in-migration from people living both within the United States and outside the country. The 2010 U.S. Census provides a telling indicator of this trend. The South was the nation's fastest-growing region between 2000 and 2010, growing at 14.3 percent, followed by the West with a 13.8 percent increase, the Midwest with a 3.9 percent increase, and the Northeast with a 3.2 percent increase (Mackun and Wilson 2011).[2] While it is certainly inevitable that these changes will have some effect on southern identity, the evidence we have accumulated in this book leads us to predict that southern identity will remain an important and vital construct. Like Reed (1983, 110), we believe "that regional categories will remain a useful way to organize the data of experience, not just for survey researchers (who always include region as a 'face-sheet datum') but for ordinary Americans who have occasion to interact with people from different regions."

Identity serves a purpose and helps connect people to their communities. In an increasingly globalized world, humans will look toward regional and local communities to fulfill the primal need to connect with people and places. In addition, the increasing globalization will give southerners more opportunities for social comparison. As we noted earlier in this chapter, we certainly saw evidence of this phenomenon in the focus groups. For many participants, the first time they really reflected on their southern identity was when they traveled to another part of the country or when they interacted with people from outside the region. The tendency for social comparison caused Reed to argue that identity would perhaps be most important to the more cosmopolitan of southerners. "Rather it is those who are most modern in background and experience—the increasing proportion of Southerners who live in cities, who have had a good deal of education, who travel and watch television and read, who do business with non-southerners—who (if they are not lost to the regional group altogether) are most likely to think in regional terms, to categorize themselves and others as 'Southerners' and 'non-Southerners,' and to believe that they may know what that means" (Reed 1983, 111). Like most social constructs, southern identity has shown an ability to evolve and change over time.

One factor that has the potential to make southern identity less attractive for minorities in the South is the recent tendency for conservatives to be more likely than moderates and liberals to call themselves southerners. If southern identity moves away from shared culture and is focused more on conservative politics—the concept could once again become something that excludes large portions of southern society.

Some of our best clues for answering questions about the future of southern identity also come from examining the opinions of younger southerners. Looking back to our survey results, we found no evidence that age had any effect on southern identity. But, we did discover that the younger focus group participants were often the most ardent defenders of the South, even lamenting the ways that southerners are portrayed on social media. This younger group of southerners will certainly play a major role in shaping the future of southern identity and determine whether the concept will evolve and still have meaning.

Understanding southern identity in the future will also require accounting for the overlapping identities that will continue to define the region. As we mentioned in the introduction, most people—even southerners—are geographically situated in multiple regions. Residents of the southeastern corner of Louisiana, for example, may identify with America, the South, Louisiana, southeastern Louisiana, Cajun Country, or the Gulf Coast— creating a "multi-scalar and web-like" patchwork of overlapping identities (McEwen 2004, 55). In this book, we have consciously avoided considering how these overlapping identities interact with one another, but a complete understanding of southern identity will require making room for multiple identities. For example, if a resident of this part of Louisiana identifies strongly as "Cajun," does that necessarily mean that their southern identity is diminished as a result? Race, gender, and political orientation also likely compete with southernness for identity and may represent even more overlapping identities. Despite our primary focus on southern identity in this book, we are under no illusion that southernness is as important to many folks as race, gender, familial lineage, or a host of other identifiers.

The future of southern identity will also, no doubt, be affected by the region's growing racial and ethnic diversity. The Latino population in Florida and Texas exceeds 4 million, and in Virginia, North Carolina, and Georgia, it exceeds 500,000. In fact, Mississippi is the only southern state where the

Latino population sits at less than 100,000 (Barreto and Segura 2014, 20). While many have speculated about the electoral importance of this group of southerners, very few scholars, journalists, or commentators have explicitly considered how Latinos (many of whom are first-generation geographic southerners) do or do not identify with the region. There is evidence that Latinos seek ties to local community (Fink 2003), but we know very little about whether they connect to the South. Will Latinos become "assimilated southerners," or will they eschew regional identity for other forms of geographic identity like national origin? Do the same processes apply to Latinos, regardless of country of origin? Do they apply to Asians and other minorities who migrate to the region as well? What about Native Americans, who have occupied the region far longer than white or black geographic southerners?

This push and pull among overlapping identities will certainly shape the future of southern identity. However, southern identity has proven to be a resilient construct that helps millions of southerners understand their place in the world. We do not see that changing anytime soon.

We employ a mixed-methods approach in this book, meaning that we use a variety of research designs and data collection strategies to measure, track, and attempt to explain southern identity. We hope that by including such disparate data, we can give a variety of different perspectives—all of which reinforce our major conclusions. The downside, of course, is that it's a lot of data collection to describe. In an effort to keep the main text of the book from getting too bogged down in technical jargon, we compiled an appendix to provide more details about our methodology.

Chapter 1

We analyze 1995 Southern Focus Poll (SFP) data on food in chapter 1 as well as the 2012 American National Election Survey (ANES). The SFP results appear in table A1.1 and table A1.2, and the ANES analyses appear in table A1.3 below.

TABLE A1.1 Are foods really regional?

	Southerners	Nonsoutherners	Difference
Southern Foods			
Okra	40	11	29
Chitlins	41	11	30
Pork Rinds	14	9	5
Catfish	35	14	21
Moon Pie	14	5	9
Fried Tomatoes	16	13	3
Sweet Potato Pie	22	14	8
Boiled Peanuts	16	5	11
Nonsouthern Foods			
Kielbasa	9	17	−8
Lox	2	3	−1
Arugula	2	2	0
Venison	16	15	1
Caviar	2	2	0
N	919	491	

Note: Data are from the spring 1995 Southern Focus Polls. Entries refer to the percentage of respondents who answered that they "often" eat the food in question.

TABLE A1.2 Is there a difference between white and black food preferences in the South?

	White Southerners	Black Southerners	Difference
Southern Foods			
Okra	40	44	−4
Chitlins	40	48	−8
Pork Rinds	14	20	−6
Catfish	35	33	2
Moon Pie	14	17	−3
Fried Tomatoes	17	15	2
Sweet Potato Pie	19	47	−28
Boiled Peanuts	16	13	3
Nonsouthern Foods			
Kielbasa	10	10	0
Lox	2	2	0
Arugula	2	1	1
Venison	17	13	4
Caviar	2	3	−1
N	774	89	

Note: Data are from the spring 1995 Southern Focus Polls. Entries refer to the percentage of respondents who answered that they "often" eat the food in question.

Chapter 2

In chapter 2, we relied heavily on data from ReferenceUSA to account for the presence of "Dixie" and "Southern" businesses in 218 southern cities. The cities were selected because they represented all cities in the thirteen-state South with a population over 50,000. We were able to search the ReferenceUSA database at the main branch of the Charleston County Library and at Hunter Library at Western Carolina University.

As we noted in the text, John Shelton Reed and his research assistants combed through print phone books when he conducted his first study on naming back in the early 1970s. In our earlier work on business naming (Cooper and Knotts 2010a, 2010b) we used the website whitepages.com. In addition to the information about business names, we compiled basic demographic information from the U.S. Census Bureau about our 218 cities.

Chapter 2 also includes the results from a series of interviews with owners of both "Dixie" and "Southern" businesses. We purchased a list of these businesses from ReferenceUSA and then contacted a sample of the business owners and asked a series of

TABLE A1.3 South/Non-South feeling thermometer differences

	South	Non-South	Difference	N
Christian fundamentalists	54.3	46.2	8.1	5,294
Christians	76.8	70.2	6.6	5,472
Big business	52.8	47.4	5.4	5,457
Military	83.5	78.8	4.7	5,480
Federal government	46.9	42.3	4.6	5,447
People on welfare	53.3	49.1	4.2	5,447
Poor people	72.2	68.6	3.6	5,455
Congress	44.6	41.2	3.4	5,455
Blacks	69.6	66.2	3.4	5,450
Conservatives	55.3	52.3	3	5,394
U.S. Supreme Court	59.3	56.5	2.8	5,436
Rich people	52	49.6	2.4	5,463
Illegal immigrants	42.6	40.5	2.1	5,458
Democratic Party	56.2	54.2	2	5,856
Hispanics	67.1	65.6	1.5	5,449
Working class people	84	82.6	1.4	5,479
Republican Party	42.7	41.7	1	5,851
Middle class people	77.2	76.2	1	5,469
Whites	72.7	71.8	0.9	5,453
Tea Party	42	41.4	0.6	5,310
Asian Americans	65.9	65.6	0.3	5,451
Feminists	51.4	51.1	0.3	5,376
Liberals	48.5	48.2	0.3	5,373
Labor unions	50.4	50.7	−0.3	5,435
Mormons	49.6	50.5	−0.9	5,373
Muslims	44.2	45.6	−1.4	5,397
Catholics	60.5	62.2	−1.7	5,446
Gay men and lesbians	49.5	53.6	−4.1	5,446
Atheists	34.4	40.5	−6.1	5,379

Note: Data are from the 2012 American National Election Study. Shaded rows represent statistically significant differences at $p < .05$.

questions about their businesses, their choice of business names, and their views of the South.

In an effort to explain business naming across our cities, we computed three basic linear regression models. The models appear in table A2.1 below. The three dependent variables (D score, S score, and the difference between S score and D score) head the three columns. The three independent variables (Percent Black, Percent College Educated, and Population Density) appear on the far left of the table.

TABLE A2.1 Regression models predicting the prevalence of "Dixie" and "Southern" businesses

	D score	S score	S score–D score
Percent black	.001**	.009**	.008**
	(.000)	(.001)	(.001)
Percent college educated	−.000	.003	.003*
	(.000)	(.002)	(.002)
Population density	.000	−.000**	−.000**
	(.000)	(.000)	(.000)
N	218	218	218

Note: Entries are linear regression coefficients. Numbers in parentheses are standard errors. * $p \leq .05$ (two-tailed test), ** $p \leq .01$ (two-tailed test)

Chapter 3

In chapter 3, we rely on several different surveys to account for individual-level attitudes about southern identity and the South. Early in the chapter, we report findings from the Odum Institute's Southern Focus Polls (SFPs), which were conducted between 1992 and 2001. As we note in the text, the SFPs provide the most ambitious, consistent, and in-depth polling about the American South that has ever been conducted.

In addition to data from the SFPs, we rely primarily on two other surveys in chapter 3. First, we draw heavily on the findings of the 2011 "Southern Identity Poll," a survey we created but contracted with Public Policy Polling to conduct. The poll surveyed residents of the thirteen-state South and was in the field January 20–24, 2011. We did our best to mirror the questions and approach used in the SFPs. We include the question wording and basic frequencies below. Second, we drew on a national poll conducted by the Pew Research Center for the People and the Press to commemorate the 150th anniversary of the Civil War. This survey included responses from 1,507 adults and was in the field March 30–April 3, 2011.

Question Wording for the Southern Identity Poll (2011)

Question 1: Do you consider yourself a Southerner, or not?
Yes, No, Don't Know
Question 2: Do you think that the South today has a lot of qualities that make it special and different from the rest of the United States, or is the South pretty much like any other part of the U.S.?
South has qualities that make it special, South is pretty much like other parts of the U.S., Don't Know
Question 3: Do you think that, all things considered, the South is the best region in the United States to live in, or do you think other parts of the country are as good or better?

South is the best region, Other parts of U.S. are as good or better, No opinion

Question 4: Do you like the southern accent?

Yes, No, Don't Know

Question 5: Some people say the Confederate flag reminds them of white supremacy and racial conflict. Other people say the Confederate flag is a symbol of Southern heritage and pride. Do you think the flag is more a symbol of racial conflict or of Southern pride?

Racial conflict, Southern pride, No Opinion

Question 6: Some people in the South feel they have a lot in common with other Southerners, but others we talk to don't feel this way. How about you? Would you say you feel pretty close to Southerners in general, or that you don't feel much closer to them than you do to other people?

Feel closer to Southerners than others, Feel no closer to Southerners than to others, Feel closer to non-Southerners, Don't Know

Question 7: Not counting time spent away at school and for other temporary reasons, how long have you lived in the South?

Less than 10 years, 10 to 19 years, 20 years or more, All of your life, Don't Know

Question 8: What race do you consider yourself?

White, Black, Hispanic, Other

Question 9: What is your level of education?

Less than high school, high school, some college, college and above

Question 10: Now thinking about religion, how important would you say that religion is in your own life?

Very important, Fairly important, Not very important, Don't Know

Question 11: What is your religious affiliation?

Protestant, Catholic, Jewish, Some other religion, No religion, Don't Know

Question 12: What is your gender?

Male, Female

Question 13: Regardless of how you vote, when it comes to national politics, do you usually think of yourself as a Republican, a Democrat, an Independent, or what?

Republican, Democrat, Independent, Other, Don't Know

Question 14: When it comes to politics, do you usually think of yourself as a liberal, a conservative, a moderate, or what?

Liberal, Moderate, Conservative, Never think of self in these terms, Don't Know

Question 15: What state do you live in?

Alabama, Arkansas, Florida, Georgia, Kentucky, Louisiana, Mississippi, North Carolina, Oklahoma, South Carolina, Tennessee, Texas, Virginia

Question 16: What is your age?

The results of a series of logistic regression models that form the basis of our conclusions in chapter 3 appear in tables A3.1, A3.2, and A3.3 that follow. In table A3.1 we predict responses to the question, "do you consider yourself a southerner," where 1 = yes and 0 = no. In both of these models, we included eight independent variables:

TABLE A3.1 Logistic regression models for "Do you consider yourself a Southerner?"

	Spring Southern Focus Poll 1992	Southern Identity Poll 2011
Age	−.088	−.160
	(.137)	(.127)
Black	−.831*	−.176
	(.343)	(.306)
Conservative	−.007	.216*
	(.144)	(.111)
Deep South	.905**	1.24**
	(.259)	(.231)
Education	−.233*	−.203*
	(.110)	(.086)
Female	−.305	.016
	(.206)	(.169)
Protestant	.957**	.435*
	(.209)	(.169)
Time in South	1.43**	1.18**
	(.135)	(.110)
Constant	−3.18	−2.18**
	(.780)	(.664)
N	735	1,321

Note: Entries are logistic regression coefficients. Numbers in parentheses are standard errors. * p ≤ .05 (two-tailed test), ** p ≤ .01 (two-tailed test)

Age (1 = 18–44, 2 = 45–64, 3 = 65 and over), Black (0 = nonblack, 1 = black), Conservative (1 = liberal, 2 = moderate, 3 = conservative), Deep South (0 = residence in Peripheral South, 1 = residence in Deep South), Education (1 = less than high school, 2 = high school, 3 = some college, 4 = college and above), Female (0 = male, 1 = female), Protestant (0 = not protestant, 1 = protestant), Time in South (1 = less than 10 years, 2 = 10–19 years, 3 = all of your life).

In table A3.2 we model responses to five questions about regional pride from the 2011 Southern Identity Poll: South Is Special (0 = other places just as special, 1 = South special), South Best Region (0 = other places just as good, 1 = South best), Like Southern Accent (0 = don't like southern accent, 1 = like southern accent), Closeness to Southerners (0 = no closer to southerners, 1 = closer to southerners), and Flag about Southern Pride (0 = flag about racial conflict, 1 = flag about southern pride). Once again, we included eight independent variables: Age

TABLE A3.2 Logistic regression models for "Explaining regional pride" using Southern Identity Poll (2011)

	South Is Special	South Best Region	Like Southern Accent	Closeness to Southerners	Flag about Southern Pride
Age	−.453**	.172	−.078	−.119	.112
	(.114)	(.098)	(.130)	(.096)	(.107)
Black	−.364	−.085	−.218	−.041	−1.63**
	(.260)	(.241)	(.309)	(.235)	(.255)
Conservative	.422**	.504**	.398**	.541**	1.03**
	(.097)	(.086)	(.114)	(.085)	(.096)
Deep South	1.12**	.505**	.867**	.606**	.532**
	(.195)	(.147)	(.226)	(.142)	(.162)
Education	.000**	−.306**	−.388**	−.274**	−.170*
	(.073)	(.065)	(.089)	(.063)	(.071)
Female	.177	.127	.057	.122	−.076
	(.148)	(.130)	(.176)	(.126)	(.142)
Protestant	.491**	.227	.461**	.387**	.166
	(.151)	(.132)	(.178)	(.130)	(.146)
Time in South	.549**	.597**	.769**	.506**	.221*
	(.089)	(.084)	(.101)	(.080)	(.088)
Constant	−1.14	−2.47**	−.849	−2.09**	−1.99**
	(.531)	(.490)	(.605)	(.468)	(.510)
N	1,331	1,343	1,216	1,329	1,277

Note: Entries are logistic regression coefficients. Numbers in parentheses are standard errors. * p ≤ .05 (two-tailed test), ** p ≤ .01 (two-tailed test)

(1 = 18–44, 2 = 45–64, 3 = 65 and over), Black (0 = nonblack, 1 = black), Conservative (1 = liberal, 2 = moderate, 3 = conservative), Deep South (0 = residence in Peripheral South, 1 = residence in Deep South), Education (1 = less than high school, 2 = high school, 3 = some college, 4 = college and above), Female (0 = male, 1 = female), Protestant (0 = not protestant, 1 = protestant), Time in South (1 = less than 10 years, 2 = 10–19 years, 3 = all of your life).

In table A3.3 we model responses to five questions about regional pride from the Pew Center's 2011 national poll commemorating the 150th anniversary of the Civil War: Civil War Still Relevant (0 = civil war not relevant, 1 = civil war is relevant), Civil War States Rights (0 = slavery, 1 = states rights), Okay to Praise Conf. Leaders (0 = not okay to praise, 1 = okay to praise), Display Conf. Flag (0 = no, 1 = yes), Conf. Flag Positive Feelings (0 = not positive, 1 = positive). We included seven independent

TABLE A3.3 Logistic regression models for "Support for the Civil War and the Confederacy" using 2011 Pew Poll

	Civil War Still Relevant	Civil War States Rights	Okay to Praise Conf. Leaders	Display Conf. Flag	Conf. Flag Positive Feelings
Age	−.229**	−.450**	.035	−.560**	−.082
	(.041)	(.044)	(.045)	(.083)	(.072)
Black	−.087	−.547**	−.501**	−.002	−.244
	(.095)	(.099)	(.102)	(.146)	(.156)
Conservative	−.039	.155**	.586**	.309**	.579**
	(.041)	(.043)	(.045)	(.075)	(.076)
Education	.074*	.056	−.297**	−.612**	−.501**
	(.031)	(.032)	(.034)	(.058)	(.055)
Female	.111	.043	−.100	.276**	.073
	(.060)	(.063)	(.065)	(.108)	(.104)
Protestant	.340**	−.131*	.137*	.114	.150
	(.065)	(.067)	(.069)	(.115)	(.109)
South	−.016	.006	.319**	.848**	1.25**
	(.065)	(.068)	(.069)	(.109)	(.106)
Constant	.340	.554**	−.836**	−1.48**	−2.92**
	(.180)	(.187)	(.193)	(.312)	(.311)
N	1,375	1,245	1,239	1,437	1,414

Note: Entries are logistic regression coefficients. Numbers in parentheses are standard errors. * $p \leq .05$ (two-tailed test), ** $p \leq .01$ (two-tailed test)

variables in each of these models: Age (1 = 18–44, 2 = 45–64, 3 = 65 and over), Black (0 = nonblack, 1 = black), Conservative (1 = liberal, 2 = moderate, 3 = conservative), Education (1 = less than high school, 2 = high school, 3 = some college, 4 = college and above), Female (0 = male, 1 = female), Protestant (0 = not protestant, 1 = protestant), and South (0 = residence in non-South, 1 = residence in South).

Chapter 4

We considered a variety of strategies to complement the quantitative data we presented in chapters 2 and 3, including interviews and focus groups. Although interviews would have been useful (indeed, Thompson and Sloan [2012] learned a great deal from the interviews they conducted, and we believe that the interviews we used in chapter 2 supplemented our argument in that chapter), we soon became convinced that focus groups would help us explore the social dynamics of identity construction in more detail. While interviews are good at telling us what individual people think about without any social pressure or information from others, we wanted to learn about how southerners talked about their experiences with other southerners. This is precisely what focus groups are designed to do.

It is important to note that we conducted the focus groups ourselves. We see this as both a strength and a weakness of our data collection strategy. As the authors of this book, we were in a position to follow up on comments, dig deeper, and expand on the questions we asked. However, we concede that as two white males, we may have made it more difficult for our black participants to feel comfortable discussing some particularly uncomfortable issues. As a result, we worked hard to establish a rapport with the participants before and during the focus groups. We also opted to include some of the more sensitive questions later in the focus group.

To recruit these participants, we worked closely with a policy center at a local university. The center had previous experience recruiting focus group participants and used e-mail lists, posted flyers at community centers, and advertised using social media. In total, we talked with twenty-six participants (twelve blacks and fourteen whites). While the focus groups were not intended to be representative of the broader population, it is worth noting that we spoke with ten males (five black and five white) and sixteen females (seven black and nine white), as well as participants from a variety of ages. Each focus group lasted between seventy and ninety minutes, and participants were paid forty dollars. The script for our focus group appears below. Keep in mind, however, that probes and follow-ups varied some from group to group. There were also times when focus group participants took the discussion in directions that are not reflected below.

Focus Group Questions

Question 1:
Tell us your name, what you do for a living, and where you have lived in your life. We are particularly interested in whether you have always lived in the South or whether you have lived in other parts of the country.

Question 2:
All of you agreed to participate in a focus group of southerners. What does being a southerner mean to you?

Question 3:
How (if at all) has your identity with the region changed over time?

Question 4:
Are you ever proud to say you are a southerner? Tell us a time when you were proud to be a southerner.

Question 5:
Are you ever embarrassed to say you are a southerner? Tell us a time when you were embarrassed to be a southerner.

Question 6:
Do you think southern identity will become more or less important in the future? Why?

Question 7:

A lot of people associate the South with the Civil War. What about you? Is the Civil War an important part of how you think about the region?

Question 8:

The Confederate flag has been used as a symbol in the South. What do you think of when you see the Confederate flag?

Question 9:

Do you consider the South the best region to live in?

Question 10:

Is there anything else you would like to share with us about the South or southern identity?

Notes

Introduction

1. We define place not necessarily as a spatial representation of political boundaries, but as something that exists in both the landscape and in people's images of it.

2. Even this formulation is more complicated than it looks, as there are more definitions of the South than there are days of the week. Some define it as the eleven states of the Old Confederacy. Others add Oklahoma and Kentucky. Still others (like the U.S. Census Bureau) add in West Virginia, Maryland, and Delaware. Some even include Missouri, and many include some of these aforementioned states and exclude others. To further complicate matters, there are portions of both Utah and Ohio that are known as each state's "Dixie."

3. As strange as it may be to imagine someone living in New York proclaiming southern identity, there is clearly a market for southern identity in the Big Apple, as evidenced by the rise of restaurants like Southern Hospitality, located in the middle of Hell's Kitchen.

Chapter One

1. For example, "The American South" is mentioned in two times as many Google searches as "The American West" and thirty-eight times more frequently than "The American Midwest" or "The American Northeast."

2. It is also important to note that Cash is frequently critiqued for his focus on the experience of white southerners, as opposed to the southern experience in general.

3. However, Reed and Degler likely disagreed with Cash on many of the specifics. For a clear and succinct review of the scholarly treatment of Cash over time, see Cobb (1999, 44–77). To get a sense of the enduring power of Cash's work, look no further than the 2013 book *The New Mind of the South* by journalist Tracy Thompson.

4. Although we refer to Griffin as a sociologist, he—like Reed and many other polymaths mentioned in this book—held appointments in multiple academic departments, including sociology, history, and American studies.

5. We computed these statistics using the 2012 statewide presidential election results compiled by David Leip (2016).

6. We computed these statistics from the online directory of the U.S. Senate (2016) on June 7, 2016.

7. We computed these statistics from the online directory of the U.S. House of Representatives (2016) on June 7, 2016.

8. Reed wrote about southern distinctiveness in many books and articles. See Griffin (2001, 50–75) for an excellent review of Reed's work. For a discussion of "southern otherness," see Cobb (2005a, 9).

9. This discussion is informed by initial debates over the title of *Southern Cultures*, the preeminent journal in southern studies. Reed had argued to title the journal *Southern Culture*, but eventually ceded to his coeditor and press, and they settled on the title *Southern Cultures*—a nod to the lack of a monolithic South (Mohler 2011).

10. We borrow this phrase from Robert Putnam's (2000) discussion of the "dark side of social capital."

11. Confederate flag sales saw a similar increase in South Carolina in the midst of the 2000 flag controversy, which ultimately resulted in the removal of the flag from the South Carolina state house dome and its placement on the state house grounds (Glaser and Ryan 2013, 58).

Chapter Two

1. Almost 94 percent of the population of St. George are members of the Church of Jesus Christ of Latter-day Saints.

2. We've also examined "Dixie" and "Southern" businesses at the state level (Cooper and Knotts 2010b).

3. This technique is called "ordinary krigging" and is frequently used by geographers to interpolate data like ours (Issaks and Srivastava 1990).

4. We do not have S score data for 1998 because Alderman and Beavers collected D, but not S, scores in that year.

5. This difference is statistically significant ($p < .05$).

Chapter Three

1. Data from the Southern Focus Polls were used in at least seventy AJC articles.

2. This is not to say, of course, that there are no excellent polls that focus on southerners. Most southern states have active polling operations that ask state-specific questions. Some of these, including the University of Arkansas's Diane B. Blair Center of Southern Politics and Society and Winthrop University's Winthrop Poll, ask questions of importance to the study of southern identity.

3. It is worth mentioning a couple of small exceptions to this trend by two well-respected national surveys. From time to time, the American National Election Studies (ANES) asked people to indicate on a scale of 1 to 100 their "feelings" about southerners. The 1990 General Social Survey (GSS) also included a feeling thermometer question, asking respondents to rate white southerners. While these questions are important (indeed, we return to them later in this chapter), they address affect, not identity.

4. Southern identification in Virginia was also very similar for both men (65 percent) and women (67 percent). The percentage of southern identifiers was higher among whites (71 percent) than blacks (52 percent) in Virginia, however.

5. We found considerable evidence to support this assertion in our previous work, where we found that Kentucky is the sixth "most southern" state in the country (Cooper and Knotts 2004).

6. Women identified as southerners at a slightly higher level than men in Kentucky (74 percent of women and 69 percent of men). Among whites, the percentage of southern identifiers was 73 percent. The Kentucky poll only included two racial groups, white and "other." Among respondents identifying as "other," 59 percent identified as southerners.

7. The level of southern identification between men and women was quite similar, with 24 percent of women identifying as southerners and 22 percent of men. The poll also indicated that 24 percent of whites and 20 percent of African Americans in Missouri identified as southerners.

8. We would be remiss if we did not note that ideology and partisanship are distinct concepts. Although today the vast majority of Republicans are conservatives, and Democrats are liberals, this was not always the case. This sorting of ideology and partisanship may play a large role in the aforementioned political polarization that has fundamentally changed American politics in the last few decades.

9. In a previous study, we compared the views of southern blacks and nonsouthern blacks on the Confederate flag and discovered that southern blacks expressed even less support for the flag than nonsouthern blacks (Cooper and Knotts 2006).

Chapter Four

1. Some use this interruption of migration during the Great Depression to differentiate between the Great Migration (1910–1930) and the Second Great Migration (1940–1970). For the purposes of this book, however, we refer to the period from 1910 to 1970 as simply the Great Migration.

2. While urban migration was most common, a substantial number of blacks did move to the rural South as well (Falk, Hunt, and Hunt 2004).

3. This is one reason why media coverage at presidential debates influences opinion more than the debate itself.

4. These differences could be due to our different modes of evidence collection. Recall that Thompson and Sloan (2012) rely on individually conducted interviews, whereas we use focus groups. It is possible that the group dynamic inherent in a focus group created social pressure for our participants to make sure they mentioned race. Left to their own devices, they might have avoided the subject and conformed to the findings of Thompson and Sloan.

5. We recognize that there were many "Confederate battle flags," but in this chapter we are using the term to describe its most common manifestation today—the Army of Northern Virginia battle flag.

6. It is worth noting that we conducted these focus groups before the shootings at Emanuel African Methodist Episcopal Church in Charleston and the national conversation about the Confederate flag that emanated in its aftermath.

7. The Confederate battle flag was once a part of the Georgia state flag and continues to be a prominent part of the Mississippi state flag.

8. At the time that we conducted the focus groups, Jon Stewart was still hosting *The Daily Show*.

Conclusion

1. 86 percent of southern Republicans were white (2 percent were black) and 45 percent of southern Democrats were black (35 percent were white (American National Election Study 2012).

2. These trends do not appear to be subsiding. Between 2013 and 2014, six of the states with the largest numerical increase in population were states of the Old Confederacy (Texas, Florida, Georgia, North Carolina, South Carolina, and Georgia). Just these six states accounted for 45 percent of the country's growth during this one-year period (U.S. Census Bureau 2014).

References

Acharya, Avidit, Matthew Blackwell, and Maya Sen. 2016. "The Political Legacy of American Slavery." *Journal of Politics*. 78(3). DOI: 10.1086/686631.

Agiesta, Jennifer. 2015. "Poll: Majority Sees Confederate Flag as Southern Pride Symbol, Not Racist." *CNN Politics*. http://www.cnn.com/2015/07/02/politics /confederate-flag-poll-racism-southern-pride. Accessed August 16, 2015.

Alderman, Derek H. 2006. "Naming Streets for Martin Luther King, Jr.: No Easy Road." In *Landscape and Race in the United States*, edited by Richard H. Schein, 215–238. New York: Routledge.

———. 2008. "Place, Naming, and the Interpretation of Cultural Landscapes." In *The Ashgate Research Companion to Heritage and Identity*, edited by Brian Graham and Peter Howard, 195–213. Burlington, VT: Ashgate Publishing Company.

Alderman, Derek H., and Donna Alderman. 2001. "Kudzu: A Tale of Two Vines." *Southern Cultures* 7 (3): 49–64.

Alderman, Derek H., and Robert Maxwell Beavers. 1999. "Heart of Dixie Revisited: An Update on the Geography of Naming in the American South." *Southeastern Geographer* 39 (2): 190–205.

Allen, Mike. 2005. "RNC Chief to Say It Was 'Wrong' to Exploit Racial Conflict for Votes." *Washington Post*, July 14. http://www.washingtonpost.com/wp-dyn /content/article/2005/07/13/AR2005071302342.html. Accessed June 2, 2015.

Ambinakudige, Shrinidhi. 2009. "Revisiting 'The South' and 'Dixie': Delineating Vernacular Regions using GIS." *Southeastern Geographer* 49 (3): 240–250.

American National Election Studies (ANES). 2012. ANES 2012 Times Series Study. Ann Arbor, MI: Inter-University Consortium for Political and Social Research.

Ashmore, Harry S. 1958. *An Epitaph for Dixie*. New York: W. W. Norton and Company.

Barreto, Matt, and Gary M. Segura. 2014. *Latino America: How America's Most Dynamic Population Is Poised to Transform the Politics of the Nation*. New York: Public Affairs.

Bass, Jack, and Marilyn W. Thompson. 1998. *Ol' Strom: An Unauthorized Biography of Strom Thurmond*. Atlanta, Ga.: Longstreet Press, Inc.

Berg, Lawrence D., and Robin A. Kearns. 1996. "Naming as Norming: 'Race', Gender, and the Identity Politics of Naming Places in Aotearoa/New Zealand." *Environment and Planning D: Society and Space* 14 (1): 99–122.

Bernard, Richard M. 1989. "Sunbelt South." In *Encyclopedia of Southern Culture*, edited by Charles R. Wilson and William Ferris, 732. Chapel Hill: University of North Carolina Press.

Black, Earl, and Merle Black. 1987. *Politics and Society in the South*. Cambridge, Mass.: Harvard University Press.

———. 2002. *The Rise of Southern Republicans*. Cambridge, Mass.: Harvard University Press.

———. 2007. *Divided America: The Ferocious Power Struggle in American Politics*. New York: Simon & Schuster.

Black, Merle, and John Shelton Reed. 1982. "Blacks and Southerners: A Research Note." *Journal of Politics* 44 (1): 165–171.

Brown, Alton. 2014. "Interview with Alton Brown." *Garden & Gun*, August/ September. http://gardenandgun.com/article/gg-interview-alton-brown. Accessed on June 6, 2016.

Carlton, David L. 2001. "Rethinking Southern History." *Southern Cultures* 7 (1): 38–49.

Carter, Dan T. 1995. *The Politics of Rage: George Wallace, the Origins of the New Conservatism, and the Transformation of American Politics*. New York: Simon & Schuster.

Cash, Wilbur J. (1941) 1991. *The Mind of the South*. New York: Vintage Books Edition.

Ceuppens, Bambi, and Marie-Claire Foblets. 2008. "The Flemish Case: A Monolingual Region in a Multilingual Federal State," in *Regional Identity and Diversity in Europe: Experience in Wales, Silesia, and Flanders*, edited by David M. Smith and Enid Wistrich, 102–158. London: The Federal Trust for Research and Education.

Change.org. 2013. "Dixie State College: Choose an Appropriate Name for the University." A petition by Dannelle Larsen-Rife. http://www.change.org /petitions/dixie-state-college-choose-an-appropriate-name-for-the-university. Accessed June 3, 2014.

Chasmar, Jessica. 2014. "Sons of Confederate Veterans Win Battle over License Plates." *Washington Times*, February 19. http://www.washingtontimes.com/news /2014/feb/19/sons-confederate-veterans-win-battle-over-license-/. Accessed June 9, 2014.

Clark, John A. 1997. "Explaining Elite Attitudes on the Georgia Flag." *American Politics Quarterly* 25 (4): 482–496.

Clyburn, James E. 2014. *Blessed Experiences: Genuinely Southern, Proudly Black*. Columbia: University of South Carolina Press.

Cobb, James C. 1999. *Redefining Southern Culture: Mind and Identity in the Modern South*. Athens: University of Georgia Press.

———. 2005a. *Away Down South: A History of Southern Identity*. New York: Oxford University Press.

———. 2005b. *The Brown Decision, Jim Crow, and Southern Identity*. Athens: University of Georgia Press.

Cohen, Dov, Richard E. Nisbett, Brian F. Bowdle, and Norbert Schwarz. 1996. "Insult, Aggression, and the Southern Culture of Honor: An 'Experimental Ethnography.'" *Journal of Personality and Social Psychology* 70 (5): 945–960.

Cohen, Dov, Joseph Vandello, Sylvia Puente, and Adrian Rantilla. 1999. "'When You Call Me That, Smile!' How Norms for Politeness, Interaction Styles, and Aggression Work Together in Southern Culture." *Social Psychology Quarterly* 62 (3): 257–275.

Collins, Scott. 2013. "Paula Deen Blames Southern Upbringing for N-Word Controversy." *Los Angeles Times*, June 20. http://articles.latimes.com/2013/jun/20

/entertainment/la-et-st-paula-deen-blames-southern-upbringing-for-nword
-controversy-20130620.

Colurso, Mary. 2013. "Blast from the Past: Patterson Hood Talks about 'Southern
Rock Opera.'" *Alabama Media Group*, January 8. http://www.al.com
/entertainment/index.ssf/2013/01/blast_from_the_past_patterson.html. Accessed
July 28, 2013.

Cooper, Christopher A., and H. Gibbs Knotts. 2004. "Defining Dixie: A State-
Level Measure of the Modern Political South." *American Review of Politics* 25
(Summer): 25–40.

———. 2006. "Region, Race, and Support for the South Carolina Confederate Flag."
Social Science Quarterly 87 (1): 142–154.

———. 2010a. "'Declining Dixie': Regional Identification in the Modern American
South." *Social Forces* 88 (3): 1083–1101.

———. 2010b. "South Polls: Rethinking the Boundaries of the South." *Southern
Cultures* 16 (4): 72–88.

———. 2012. "Love 'Em or Hate 'Em? Changing Racial and Regional Differences in
Opinions toward Southerners, 1964–2008." *Social Science Quarterly* 93 (1): 58–75.

———. 2013. "Overlapping Identities in the American South." *Social Science Journal*
50 (1): 6–12.

———. 2014. "Partisan Change in Southern State Legislatures, 1953–2013." *Southern
Cultures* 20 (2): 75–89.

Coski, John M. 2005. *The Confederate Battle Flag: American's Most Embattled Emblem.*
Cambridge, Mass.: Harvard University Press.

Crespino, Joseph. 2012. *Strom Thurmond's America.* New York: Hill and Wang.

Davis, Janel. 2014. "Rick Allen Upsets John Barrow for Georgia Congressional
Seat." *Atlanta Journal-Constitution*, November 4. http://www.ajc.com/news/news
/state-regional-govt-politics/rick-allen-upsets-john-barrow-for-georgia/nhzbx/.
Accessed June 7, 2016.

Degler, Carl N. 1997. *Place over Time: The Continuity of Southern Distinctiveness.*
Athens: University of Georgia Press.

Douthat, Ross. 2007. "Crisis of Faith." *Atlantic*, July/August. http://www.theatlantic
.com/magazine/archive/2007/07/crises-of-faith/305967/. Accessed December 30,
2012.

Dwyer, Owen J., and Derek H. Alderman. 2008. *Civil Rights Memorials and the
Geography of Memory.* Athens: University of Georgia Press.

Edelman, Murray. 1964. *The Symbolic Uses of Politics.* Urbana: University of Illinois
Press.

Ehrlinger, Joyce, E. Ashby Plant, Richard P. Eibach, Corey J. Columb, Joanna L.
Goplen, Jonathan W. Kintsman, and David A. Butz. 2011. "How Exposure to the
Confederate Flag Affects Willingness to Vote for Barack Obama." *Political
Psychology* 32 (1): 131–146.

Ennis, Sharon R., Merarys Rios-Vargas, and Nora G. Albert. 2011. *The Hispanic
Population 2010.* 2010 Census Briefs, C2010BR-04. Washington, D.C.: U.S. Census
Bureau, May. http://www.census.gov/prod/cen2010/briefs/c2010br-04.pdf.
Accessed December 17, 2014.

Eversley, Melanie. 2015. "9 Dead in Shooting at Black Church in Charleston, SC." *USA Today*, June 19. http://www.usatoday.com/story/news/nation/2015/06/17 /charleston-south-carolina-shooting/28902017/. Accessed June 23, 2015.

Falk, William W., Larry L. Hunt, and Matthew O. Hunt. 2004. "Return Migrations of African-Americans to the South: Reclaiming a Land of Promise, Going Home, or Both? *Rural Sociology* 69: 490–509.

Faulkner, William. 1950. *Requiem for a Nun*. New York: Random House.

Ferris, Marcie Cohen. 2009. "The Edible South." *Southern Cultures* 15 (4): 3–27.

Fink, Leon. 2003. *The Maya of Morganton: Work and Community in the Nuevo New South*. Chapel Hill: University of North Carolina Press.

Frederickson, Keri. 2001. *The Dixiecrat Revolt and the End of the Solid South, 1932–1968*. Chapel Hill, NC: University of North Carolina Press.

Frey, William H. 2001. "Census 2000 Shows Large Black Return to the South, Reinforcing the Region's 'White-Black' Demographic Profile." *Population Studies Center Research Report*, no. 01–473. Ann Arbor: University of Michigan.

———. 2004. *The New Great Migration: Black Americans Return to the South, 1965–2000*. Living Cities Census Series. Washington, D.C.: Brookings Institution.

Glaser, James M., and Timothy J. Ryan. 2013. *Changing Minds If Not Hearts: Political Remedies for Racial Conflict*. Philadelphia: University of Pennsylvania Press.

Glenn, Norval D., and J. L. Simmons. 1967. "Are Regional Cultural Differences Diminishing?" *Public Opinion Quarterly* 31 (2): 176–193.

Goldfield, David. 2002. *Still Fighting the Civil War: The American South and Southern History*. Baton Rouge: Louisiana State University Press.

Gordon, Pat. 1981. "Applebee's: Nostalgia on Six-Lane Highway." *Dekalb Neighbor*. February 18.

Gosling, Sam. 2008. *Snoop: What Your Stuff Says about You*. New York: Basic Books.

Governing 2016. "Homegrown, Native Population totals for U.S. States, Cities." http://www.governing.com/gov-data/census-migration-homegrown -populations-for-cities-states.html. Accessed June 16, 2016.

Grady, Henry. 1886. "The New South Speech." http://www.anselm.edu/academic /history/hdubrulle/CivWar/text/documents/doc54.htm. Accessed November 11, 2014.

Green, Donald, Bradley Palmquist, and Eric Schickler. 2002. *Partisan Hearts and Minds: Political Parties and the Social Identity of Voters*. New Haven, Conn.: Yale University Press.

Griffin, Larry J. 2001. "The Promise of a Sociology of the South." *Southern Cultures* 7 (1): 50–75.

———. 2006. "The American South and the Self." *Southern Cultures* 12 (3): 6–28.

Griffin, Larry J., and Ashley B. Thompson. 2003. "Enough about the Disappearing South: What about the Disappearing Southerner?" *Southern Cultures* 9 (3): 51–65.

Griffin, Larry J., Ranae Jo Evanson, and Ashley B. Thompson. 2005. "Southerners All?" *Southern Cultures* 11 (1): 6–25.

Grimmett, Brian. 2013. "Legislature Approves Dixie State University Name Change." *KUER.org*. http://kuer.org/post/legislature-approves-dixie-state -university-name-change. Accessed June 3, 2014.

Hein, Virginia H. 1972. "The Image of 'A City Too Busy to Hate': Atlanta in the 1960s." *Phylon* 33 (3): 205–221.

Hogg, Michael A. 2006. "Social Identity Theory." In *Contemporary Social Psychology Theories*, edited by P. J. Burke, 111–136. Palo Alto, Calif.: Stanford University Press.

Hood, M. V., III, Quentin Kidd, and Irwin L. Morris. 2012. *The Rational Southerner: Black Mobilization, Republican Growth, and the Partisan Transformation of the American South*. New York: Oxford University Press.

Hood, Patterson. 2002. "The Three Great Alabama Icons." *Southern Rock Opera*. Lost Highway Records.

———. 2013. "The New(er) South." *The Bitter Southerner*. http://bittersoutherner .com/patterson-hood-the-newer-south/. Accessed December 10, 2014.

———. 2015. "The South's Heritage Is So Much More Than a Flag." *New York Times*, July 9.

Hunt, Larry L., Matthew O. Hunt, and William W. Falk. 2008. "Who Is Headed South? U.S. Migration Trends in Black and White, 1970–2000." *Social Forces* 87: 95–119.

Hunt, Matthew O., Larry L. Hunt, and William W. Falk. 2013. "Twenty-First-Century Trends in Black Migration to the U.S. South: Demographic and Subjective Predictors." *Social Science Quarterly* 94: 1398–1413.

Hurlbert, Jeanne S. 1989. "The Southern Region: A Test of the Hypothesis of Cultural Distinctiveness." *Sociological Quarterly* 30 (2): 245–266.

Inscoe, John. 2011. *Writing the South through the Self: Explorations in Southern Autobiography*. Athens: University of Georgia Press.

Issaks, Edward H., and R. Mohan Srivastava. 1990. *An Introduction to Applied Geostatistics*. New York: Oxford University Press.

Iyengar, Shanto, and Sean J. Westwood. 2015. "Fear and Loathing across Party Lines: New Evidence on Group Polarization." *American Journal of Political Science* 59: 690–707.

Key, V. O. 1949. *Southern Politics in State and Nation*. New York: Alfred A. Knopf.

Kinzler, Katherine D., and Jasmine M. DeJesus. 2013. "Northern = Smart and Southern = Nice: The Development of Accent Attitudes in the United States." *Quarterly Journal of Experimental Psychology* 66 (6): 1146–1158.

Kotkin, Joel. 2013. "How the South Will Rise to Power Again." *Forbes*, January 31. http://www.forbes.com/sites/joelkotkin/2013/01/31/how-the-south-will-rise-to -power-again/#7201b06c4924. Accessed February 27, 2016.

Kruse, Kevin. 2007. *White Flight: Atlanta and the Making of Modern Atlanta*. Princeton, N.J.: Princeton University Press.

Lamare, James, J. L. Polinard, Joseph Stewart, and Robert D. Wrinkle. 2012. "Buenas Dias, Ya'll: Latinos in the South." In *The Oxford Handbook of Southern Politics*, edited by Charles S. Bullock and Mark J. Rozell, 204–215. New York: Oxford University Press.

Lamis, Alexander P. 1999. *Southern Politics in the 1990s*. Baton Rouge: Louisiana State University Press.

Lassiter, Matthew. D. 2007. *The Silent Majority: Suburban Politics in the Sunbelt South*. Princeton, N.J.: Princeton University Press.

Latshaw, Beth A. 2009. "Food for Thought: Race, Region, Identity, and Foodways in the American South." *Southern Cultures* 15 (4): 106–128.

Lee, Matt, and Ted Lee. 2006. "Bobby Flay in Love with Savannah." *Food & Wine*, May. http://www.foodandwine.com/articles/bobby-flay-in-love-with-savannah. Accessed July 28, 2013.

Leip, David. 2016. *Dave Leip's Atlas of U.S. Presidential Elections.* http://uselectionatlas.org. Accessed June 7, 2016.

Lemann, Nicholas. 1991. *The Promised Land: The Great Migration and How It Changed America.* New York: Knopf.

Light, Duncan. 2004. "Street Names in Bucharest, 1990–1997: Exploring Modern Historical Geographies of Post Socialist Change." *Journal of Historical Geography* 30 (1): 154–172.

Lloyd, Richard. 2012. "Urbanization and the Southern United States." *Annual Review of Sociology* 38: 483–506.

Mackun, Paul, and Steven Wilson. 2011. *Population Distribution and Change: 2000 to 2010.* 2010 Census Briefs, C2010BR-01. Washington, D.C.: U.S. Census Bureau, March. http://www.census.gov/prod/cen2010/briefs/c2010br-01.pdf. Accessed December 16, 2014.

Maffly, Brian. 2012. "Utah's Dixie Was Steeped in Salve Culture, Historians Say." *Salt Lake Tribune.* December 10. http://www.sltrib.com/sltrib/news/55424505-78/covington-utah-county-cotton.html.csp. Accessed June 3, 2014.

Mann, Jennifer E. 2010. "The Coast as a Vernacular Region." Masters thesis, East Carolina University. http://thescholarship.ecu.edu/handle/10342/2897. Accessed February 28, 2016.

Marcus, George E., W. Russell Neuman, and Michael MacKuen. 2000. *Affective Intelligence and Political Judgment.* Chicago, IL: University of Chicago Press.

McEwen, John W. 2014. "Louisiana: Apprehending a Complex Web of Vernacular Regional Geography." *Southeastern Geographer* 54 (1): 55–71.

Mickey, Robert. 2015. *Paths out of Dixie: The Democratization of Authoritarian Enclaves in America's Deep South, 1944–1972.* Princeton, N.J.: Princeton University Press.

Mitchell, Margaret. 1936. *Gone with the Wind.* New York: Macmillan.

Mitchelson, Matthew, Derek Alderman, and Jeff Popke. 2007. "Branded: The Economic Geographies of MLK Streets." *Social Science Quarterly* 88 (1): 120–145.

Mixon, Wayne. 1989. "New South Myth." In *Encyclopedia of Southern Culture*, edited by Charles R. Wilson and William Ferris, 1113. Chapel Hill: University of North Carolina Press.

Mohler, Albert. 2011. "The Persistence of Place: A Conversation with John Shelton Reed." AlbertMohler.com. http://www.albertmohler.com/2011/02/24/the-persistence-of-place-a-conversation-with-john-shelton-reed/. Accessed on September 6, 2013.

Montgomery, Michael. 1993. "The Southern Accent—Alive and Well." *Southern Cultures* 1 (1): 47–64.

Orey, Byron D'Andra. 2004. "White Racial Attitudes and Support for the Mississippi State Flag." *American Politics Research* 32 (1): 102–116.

Paasi, Anssi. 2003. "Region and Place: Regional Identity in Question." *Progress in Human Geography* 27 (4): 475–485.

Patterson, James T. 2001. *Brown v. Board of Education: A Civil Rights Milestone and Its Troubled Legacy*. New York: Oxford University Press.

Phillips, Kevin. 1969. *The Emerging Republican Majority*. New York: Arlington House.

Phillips, Ulrich B. 1928. "The Central Theme of Southern History." *American Historical Review* 34 (1): 30–43.

Pierce, Dan. 2001. "The Most Southern Sport on Earth: NASCAR and the Unions." *Southern Cultures* 7 (2): 8–33.

Powledge, Fred. 1979. *Journeys through the South: A Rediscovery*. New York: Vanguard Press.

Public Policy Polling. 2011. "Virginia Survey Results." http://www.publicpolicypolling .com/pdf/2011/PPP_Release_VA_1215424.pdf. Accessed December 26, 2012.

———. 2012. "Missouri Survey Results." http://www.publicpolicypolling.com/pdf /2011/PPP_Release_MO_060112.pdf. Accessed December 26, 2012.

———. 2013. "Kentucky Survey Results." http://www.publicpolicypolling.com/pdf /2011/PPP_Release_KY_411.pdf. Accessed August 16, 2015.

Putnam, Robert D. 2000. *Bowling Alone: The Collapse and Revival of American Community*. New York: Simon & Schuster.

Reed, John Shelton. 1972. *The Enduring South: Subcultural Persistence in Mass Society*. Lexington, Mass.: DC Heath & Company.

———. 1973. "'The Cardinal Test of a Southerner:' Not Race But Geography." *Public Opinion Quarterly* 37 (2): 232–240.

———. 1976. "The Heart of Dixie: An Essay in Folk Geography." *Social Forces* 54 (4): 925–939.

———. 1982. *One South: An Ethnic Approach to Regional Culture*. Baton Rouge: Louisiana State University Press.

———. 1983. *Southerners: The Social Psychology of Sectionalism*. Chapel Hill: University of North Carolina Press.

———. 1993. *My Tears Spoiled My Aim: And Other Reflections on Southern Culture*. San Diego, Calif.: Harvest Books.

———. 1995. "Pass the Grits." *Southern Cultures* 1 (4): 529–531.

———. 1996. "Happy New Year." *Southern Cultures* 2 (3/4): 421–423.

———. 1997. "Mama'nem." *Southern Cultures* 3 (2): 96–98.

———. 1999. "Living and Dying in Dixie." *Southern Cultures* 5 (1): 106.

———. 2011. E-mail interview, March 17.

Reed, John Shelton, James Kohls, and Carol Hanchette. 1990. "The Dissolution of Dixie and the Changing Shape of the South." *Social Forces* 69 (1): 221–233.

Reingold, Beth, and Richard S. Wike. 1998. "Confederate Symbols, Southern Identity, and Racial Attitudes: The Case of the Georgia State Flag." *Social Science Quarterly* 79 (3): 568–580.

Rice, Tom W., William P. McLean, and Amy J. Larsen. 2002. "Southern Distinctiveness over Time 1972–2000." *American Review of Politics* 23 (Spring–Summer): 193–220.

Rose-Redwood, Reuben S. 2008. "From Number to Name: Symbolic Capital, Places of Memory, and the Politics of Renaming in New York City." *Social and Cultural Geography* 9 (4): 431–452.

Shortridge, James R. 1987. "Changing Usage of Four American Regional Labels." *Annals of the Association of American Geographers* 77 (3): 325–336.

Sorenson Advertising. 2013. "Dixie State College of Utah Research Report." https://old .dixie.edu/namechange/File/DSC-Research-Report-January-9-2013.pdf. Accessed June 6, 2016.

Southern Focus Polls. 2016. The Odum Institute. http://www.odum.unc.edu/odum /contentSubpage.jsp?nodeid=82. Accessed June 6, 2016.

Stets, Jan E., and Peter J. Burke. 2000. "Identity Theory and Social Identity Theory." *Social Psychology Quarterly* 63 (3): 224–237.

Stewart, Nikita, and Richard Pérez-Peña. 2015. "In Charleston, Raw Emotion at Hearing for Suspect in Church Shooting." *New York Times*, June 19. http://www .nytimes.com/2015/06/20/us/charleston-shooting-dylann-storm-roof.html?_r=0. Accessed June 14, 2016.

Swann v. Charlotte-Mecklenburg Board of Education. 1971. 402 U.S. 1.

Tajfel, Henri. 1972. "Social Categorization." (English manuscript of "La catégorisation sociale.") In *Introduction à la Psychologie Sociale*, edited by S. Moscovici, 1: 272–302. Paris: Larousse.

Thompson, Ashley B., and Melissa M. Sloan. 2012. "Race as Region, Region as Race: How Black and White Southerners Understand Their Regional Identities." *Southern Cultures* 18 (4): 72–95.

Thompson, Chuck. 2012. *Better Off Without 'Em: A Northern Manifesto for Southern Secession*. New York: Simon & Schuster.

Thompson, Tracy. 2013. *The New Mind of the South*. New York: Simon & Schuster.

Tindall, George B. 1960. "The Status and Future of Regionalism—A Symposium." *Journal of Southern History* 26: 22–24.

———. 1976. *The Ethnic Southerners*. Baton Rouge: Louisiana State University Press.

———. 1989. "Mythic South." In *Encyclopedia of Southern Culture*, edited by Charles R. Wilson and William Ferris, 1097. Chapel Hill: University of North Carolina Press.

Tissenbaum, Marc. 2015. "A Southern Gentleman in the Old Northwest: Patterson Hood on Moving to Portland and Being Inescapably Southern." *Paste Magazine*. July 21. https://www.pastemagazine.com/articles/2015/07/a-southern-gentleman -in-the-old-northwest-patterso.html. Accessed June 22, 2016.

Trethewey, Natasha. 2006. *Native Guard*. Boston, Mass.: Houghton Mifflin Company.

Turner, Daniel Cross. 2013. "Southern Crossings: An Interview with Natasha Trethewey." *Waccamaw: A Journal of Contemporary Literature* 11 (Spring). http://www.archived.waccamawjournal.com/pages.php?x=324. Accessed August 25, 2013.

U.S. Census Bureau. 2014. "Florida Passes New York to Become the Nation's Third Most Populous State." *Census Bureau Reports*, CB14-232, December 23. https://www .census.gov/newsroom/press-releases/2014/cb14-232.html. Accessed February 28, 2016.

———. 2015. "State Totals: Vintage 2015." *Population Estimates*. http://www.census .gov/popest/data/state/totals/2015/. Accessed February 27, 2016.

U.S. House of Representatives. 2016. "Directory of Representatives." http://www
.house.gov/representatives/. Accessed June 7, 2016.

U.S. Senate. 2016. "Senators of the 114th Congress." http://www.senate.gov
/senators/contact/. Accessed June 7, 2016.

Valentino, Nicholas A., and David O. Sears. 2005. "Old Times There Are Not
Forgotten: Race and Partisan Realignment in the Contemporary South."
American Journal of Political Science 49: 672–688.

Walker, Hunter. 2013. "Paula Deen on Her Dream 'Southern Plantation
Wedding.'" *Talking Points Memo.* http://tpmdc.talkingpointsmemo.com/2013/06
/paula-deen-racial.php. Accessed August 23, 2013.

Wallace, George C. 1963. "1963 Inaugural Address." Alabama Department of
Archives and History. http://digital.archives.alabama.gov/cdm/singleitem
/collection/voices/id/2952/rec/5. Accessed December 15, 2014.

Walsh, Katherine Cramer. 2012. "Putting Inequality in Its Place: Rural
Consciousness and the Power of Perspective." *American Political Science Review*
106: 517–532.

Watts, Rebecca Bridges. 2008. *Contemporary Southern Identity: Community through
Controversy.* Oxford: University of Mississippi Press.

Weissert, Will. 2011. "Rick Perry Fought Removal of Confederate Symbols in
2000." *Dallas News.com*, October 4. http://www.dallasnews.com/news/politics
/perry-watch/headlines/20111004-rick-perry-fought-removal-of-confederate
-symbols-in-2000.ece. Accessed June 9, 2014.

Westbrook, John T. 1957. "Twilight of Southern Regionalism." *Southwest Review* 42
(Summer): 231–234.

Whitehurst, Lindsay. 2013a. "Dixie May Apologize for Past Confederate, Blackface
Imagery." *Salt Lake Tribute*, January 12. http://www.sltrib.com/sltrib/news
/55613643-78/dixie-state-college-confederate.html.csp. Accessed June 3, 2014.

———. 2013b. "Dixie State College Keeping Its Name Amid Controversy." *Salt Lake
Tribune*, January 18. http://www.sltrib.com/sltrib/news/55657801-78/dixie
-university-board-george.html.csp. Accessed June 3, 2014.

Williams, Juan. 2004. "Reagan, the South, and Civil Rights." National Public Radio.
http://www.npr.org/templates/story/story.php?storyId=1953700. Accessed
December 15, 2014.

William Winter Institute. 2015. "About Us." http://winterinstitute.org/about-us/.
Accessed August 30, 2015.

Williamson, Joel. 1984. *The Crucible of Race: Black-White Relations in the American
South since Emancipation.* New York: Oxford University Press.

Woodward, C. Vann. 1958. "The Search for Southern Identity." *Virginia Quarterly
Review* 34 (Summer): 321–328.

Zelinsky, Wilbur. 1980. "North American's Vernacular Regions." *Annals of the
Association of American Geographers* 70 (1): 1–16.

———. 1988. *Nation into State: The Shifting Symbolic Foundations of American
Nationalism.* Chapel Hill: University of North Carolina Press.

Index

Acharya, Avidit, 22
Alabama, 1, 11, 25, 36, 38, 41–42, 46,
    55–57, 67
Alderman, Derek, 37
Ambinakudige, Shrinidhi, 41
American National Election Studies
    (ANES), 21
Appalachian, 14
Applebee's, 48
Arkansas, 36, 41–42, 56
Ashmore, Harry, 4
Assimilated southerners, 29, 59, 91–92,
    105
Atwater, Lee, 26–27

Bagley, Will, 31
Barrow, John, 20
Beavers, Robert Maxwell, 37
Bentley, Robert, 11
Berg, Lawrence, 34
Black, Earl, 20
Black, Merle, 20
Black southerners: food, 19; migration,
    69; and opinions from focus group
    participants about the Civil War, 86;
    and opinions from focus group
    participants about the Confederate
    flag, 88; and opinions from focus
    groups participants about family,
    80; and opinions from focus group
    participants about food, 80; and
    opinions from focus group partici-
    pants about race relations, 82; and
    opinions from focus group partici-
    pants about southern identity, 81;
    southern identity, 11, 13, 23, 30, 51–52;
    southern pride, 66
Blackwell, Matthew, 22

Brown, Alton, 19, 80
Bryant, Bear, 1
Business names: indicators of southern
    identity, 7, 17, 37, 39, 47–49, 108–9;
    indicators of the geographic South,
    40, 42, 47; indicators of the resilience
    of southern identity, 94, 96; and
    research design, 33–34; state-level
    indicators of southern identity, 55–56

Cajun, 104
Calhoun, John, 11
Caplin, Steven, 32
Cary, North Carolina, 48
Cash, W. J., 15, 85, 117
Census South, 2, 17, 24
Changing identity, 91–93
Charleston church shooting, 5, 10–12,
    62–63, 97, 119
Civil rights movement, 13, 100
Civil War, 15; connection to the Old
    South, 35–36; effects of today, 95; and
    opinions from focus group partici-
    pants, 71–72, 85–87; and public
    opinion, 50, 64–67
Clyburn, James, 1–2, 66, 96
Cobb, James, 4, 16, 23, 27–28, 51, 101
Cochran, Thad, 11
Cohen, Dov, 17
Confederacy, 26, 31, 39, 49, 50, 53–54,
    65, 87
Confederate flag: changing attitudes
    about, 4–6, 98; and the Charleston
    shooting, 10–11, 97; dark side of
    southern identity, 25, 27; and
    opinions from focus group partici-
    pants, 71–72, 87–89; as a political
    symbol, 13; re-Confederatization, 37;

Confederate flag (cont.)
    public opinion of, 62–67; racial
    division, 95
Conflicted southerner, 81–82

Daily Show (The), 90
De-Confederatization, 37–38
Deen, Paula, 1–2, 66, 96
Defending the South, 72, 90–91
Degler, Carl, 15, 21, 117
Delaware, 14
Democratic Party, 26, 101
Dixie, 4–5
Dixie business names, 7–8, 35–48, 55
Dixiecrats, 13, 25, 35
Dixie State College, 31–33, 47
Dukes of Hazard, 90

Emanuel African Methodist Episcopal
    (AME) Church, 10–11, 63, 119
Ethnic group(s): southerners as, 22–23,
    25; southern identification among,
    105

Facebook, 89
Family, 46, 73, 78–80
Ferris, Marcie Cohen, 18
Flay, Bobby, 19–20
Florida: changing demographics, 104;
    D scores, 36; intraregional differ-
    ences, 67; S scores, 38, 42; southern
    identification, 55–56; and Winn
    Dixie, 40

Gamble, Derrick, 97
Garden and Gun, 16
Georgia: changing demographics, 104;
    Confederate flag, 62, 119n7, 120n2;
    D scores, 36–38, 41–42; food, 19–20,
    48; and the rural South, 76; S scores,
    42; southern identification, 56
Goldfield, David, 24, 86
Goldwater, Barry, 26
Gone with the Wind, 35, 74, 90
Gosling, Sam, 34

Grady, Henry, 35
Grant, Susan-Mary, 27
Griffin, Larry, 6, 15, 28–29, 61–62, 117

Haley, Nikki, 11
Hanchette, Carol, 37
Hood, Patterson, 1–2, 5, 11–12, 66, 96
Hurlbert, Jeanne, 21
Husk, 16

Inscoe, John, 15

Kearns, Robin, 34
Kentucky, 36, 39, 49, 54–56, 117–19
Key, V.O., 20, 44, 58, 85
King, Jr., Martin Luther, 34
Kohls, James, 37
Ku Klux Klan, 64, 87, 92

Lamare, James, 24
Lapsed southerners, 29, 59
Latinos, 24–25, 104–5
Levine, Lawrence, 28
Lewin, Kurt, 28
Louisiana, 36–37, 41–42, 56, 67, 104

Maryland, 36
McCrory, Pat, 11
McGovern, George, 26
Mehlman, Ken, 27
Migrants from South, 24, 69, 119
Migrants to South: assimilated south-
    erners, 29; future of southern
    identity, 103; in historical perspec-
    tive, 69, 119n1; increasing numbers, 2;
    politics, 20; southern distinctiveness,
    48; southern identity, 59
Mississippi: Center for the Study of
    Southern Culture, 16; Confederate
    flag, 11, 62, 119n7; demographics,
    104–105; and D scores, 36–39;
    intraregional differences, 67; and
    southern identity, 5, 41–42, 55–57
Mississippi, University of, 16, 37
Missouri, 36, 54, 117, 119

Mitchell, Margaret, 35
Mitchell, Pamma, 49–50
Modernization, 3, 53
Montgomery, Michael, 77

National Association for the Advance-
    ment of Colored People (NAACP),
    31, 33, 37
National Association of Stock Car
    Auto Racing (NASCAR), 18
New South, 35–37, 42–45, 68
New southerner, 98–99
New York, 5, 19, 75, 77, 92, 117
New York Times, 3, 11, 24, 90
Nixon, Richard, 13, 26
Norfolk Southern, 45
North Carolina: demographic change,
    104, 120n2; D scores, 36–38; overlap-
    ping identities, 14–15; survey data on
    southern identification, 52–53, 56
North Carolina, University of (Chapel
    Hill), 49
Northerners, 46, 74, 81, 94

Obama, Barack, 11, 27, 91
Oklahoma, 39, 42, 49, 54–56, 117
Old South, 5, 23, 35–38, 43–44, 87, 97–98

Pew Center for the People & the Press,
    50, 64
Phillips, Ulrich, 23, 95, 99
Pinckney, Clementa, 10
Place naming, 30, 33–34, 37, 55
Polinard, J.L., 24
Powledge, Fred, 24
Public Policy Polling (PPP), 50,
    53–56, 110

Race relations, 8, 22, 71–72, 82–85, 100
Rash, Ron, 6
Reagan, Ronald, 26, 101
Re-Confederatization, 37
Reed, John Shelton, 6; assimilated
    southerners, 91; business names,
    34–41, 43, 108; cultural markers of

southern identification, 17–18, 21–23;
    defining southern identification,
    14–15; Dixie, 32; the future of
    southern identity, 97, 102–3; lapsed
    southerners, 25, 59; the social psychol-
    ogy of southern identification, 28–29;
    southern distinctiveness, 117–18;
    Southern Focus Polls, 49–50, 60
Regional consciousness, 3, 27, 60,
    77–78, 102
Regional group, 7, 14, 103
Regional identification: outside the
    South, 13–15; purpose, 3; race, 23–24;
    social psychology, 27–29
Republican National Committee, 27
Republican Party: the future of
    southern identification, 101; the new
    South, 35, 59; partisan change in the
    South, 20, 57; political ideology,
    119n8; race, 120n1; the social psychol-
    ogy of partisanship, 28; southern
    state legislatures, 2; the Southern
    Strategy, 26
Re-southernization, 38
Romney, Mitt, 20
Roof, Dylann, 10–12
Rural South, 69, 76

Sanders, Felicia, 11
Sanders, Tywanza, 11
Segregation, 25–26, 35–36, 51, 58, 92
Sen, Maya, 22
Sloan, Melissa, 24, 30, 82, 114, 119n4
Smith, Leroy, 97
Social identity theory, 7–8, 13, 28–29, 102
Sons of Confederate Veterans, 37
South: cultural changes, 3; demographic
    changes, 2; suburbanization, 48
South Carolina: business names, 36, 38,
    41–42; changing demographics,
    120n2; and the Charleston church
    shooting, 5, 10–11, 97; Confederate
    flag, 62; overlapping identities,
    14–16; state level southern identi-
    fication, 56

Southern accent, 17, 62–63, 73, 77–78, 92–93
Southern Charm, 90
Southern Company, 45
Southern distinctiveness: fading, 3–4; food, 18–20; importance, 21–23; politics, 20; public opinion, 20; southern attitudes, 15
Southern Focus Polls: questions about cultural markers, 19, 74, 78, 107–8; questions about southern identity, 49–53, 58; question wording, 110; use in *Atlanta Journal Constitution* stories, 118n1
Southern food: cultural marker of southern identity, 12, 18–21, 100; focus group results, 78–80, 86; Southern Focus Poll data, 107–8; the spread of southern culture, 96
Southern hospitality, 8, 11, 73–76, 99–100, 102
Southern identity: age differences, 60; dark side, 25–27; educational differences, 59–60; future of, 103–5; ideological differences, 58, 60; in Deep South, 59–60; in Peripheral South, 59–60; politics of, 100–101; racial differences, 23–24, 58, 60, 99–100; religious differences, 59–60; sex differences, 60; social psychology, 27–29; state-by-state differences, 55–57; theory of, 101–3
Southern manners, 8, 46, 73–76, 99–100, 102
Southern pace of life, 8, 73–76, 99, 102
Southern pride: best region, 61; Confederate flag, 62; predictors of, 63; southern accent, 62; southerners, 61–62 uniqueness of the South, 61

Southern Strategy, 13, 26–27
Stewart, Joseph, 24
Sunbelt South, 35
Swann v. Charlotte Mecklenburg Board of Education, 51

Tennessee, 36, 38, 41, 55–57
Texas: and business naming, 38, 42, 55–56; and interregional differences, 67; and demographic changes, 104, 120n2
Thompson, Ashley, 24, 30, 82, 114n, 119n4
Thompson, Chuck, 16
Thompson, Tracy, 6, 117
Thurmond, Paul, 11
Thurmond, Strom, 11, 25, 35
Tindall, George, 3, 23
Traditional value orientation, 102
Trethewey, Natasha, 1–2, 66, 96
Truman, Harry, 25

Urbanization, 2, 15, 20, 27, 76

Van Zant, Ronnie, 1
Vernacular region, 13–15, 34, 48, 54
Virginia, 38, 53–56, 67, 104

Wallace, George, 1, 13, 25–26
Watts, Rebecca Bridges, 24
West Virginia, 36, 117
Wiggins, Beverly, 49–50
William Winter Center for Racial Reconsolidation, 99
Winn Dixie, 40
Wrinkle, Robert D., 24
Woodward, C. Vann, 15

Young, Brigham, 31